Reading STREET

Grade 1

Scott Foresman
Advanced
Take-Home Readers

ISBN: 0-328-16899-8
Copyright © Pearson Education, Inc.
All Rights Reserved. Printed in the United States of America. This publication,
or parts thereof, may be used with appropriate equipment to reproduce copies
for classroom use only.
7 8 9 10 V084 14 13 12 11 10 09 08

PEARSON
Scott
Foresman

Editorial Offices: Glenview, Illinois • Parsippany, New Jersey • New York, New York
Sales Offices: Boston, Massachusetts • Duluth, Georgia • Glenview, Illinois
Coppell, Texas • Sacramento, California • Mesa, Arizona

Contents

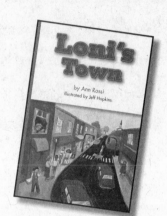

How to Use the Take-Home Leveled Readers

1. Tear out the pages for each Take-Home Leveled Reader. Make a copy for each child. Be sure to copy both sides of each page.

2. Fold the pages in half to make a booklet.

3. Staple the pages on the left-hand side.

4. Share the Take-Home Leveled Readers with children. Suggest they read these with family members.

Carlos Picks a Pet

by Ann Rossi

Genre	Comprehension Skills and Strategy
Realistic fiction	• Character • Compare and Contrast • Monitor and Fix Up

Scott Foresman Reading Street 1.1.1

PEARSON

Scott Foresman

scottforesman.com

ISBN 0-328-13144-X

9 780328 131440

90000

Vocabulary

needs

responsibility

shelter

Word count: 427

Note: The total word count includes words in the running text and headings only. Numerals and words in chapter titles, captions, labels, diagrams, charts, graphs, sidebars, and extra features are not included.

Think and Share

1. Would you want Carlos to be your friend? Why or why not? Make a web like the one below that tells about Carlos.

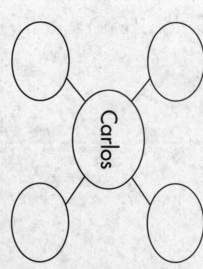

Carlos

2. If you had trouble understanding what you read, look back at the book. Why does Carlos decide that a rabbit is not the right kind of pet for him?

3. Using the words needs and responsibility, tell how Carlos picks the kind of pet that is right for him.

4. Would a cat be the right kind of pet for you? Why or why not?

A Wildlife Buffet

by Libby McCord

illustrated by Aleksey Ivanov

Genre	Comprehension Skills and Strategy
Realistic fiction	• Realism and Fantasy • Sequence • Story Structure

Scott Foresman Reading Street 1.1.5

ISBN 0-328-13156-3

9 780328 131563

90000

PEARSON

Scott Foresman

scottforesman.com

Vocabulary

habitat

hatch

survive

Word count: 373

Note: The total word count includes words in the running text and headings only. Numerals and words in chapter titles, captions, labels, diagrams, charts, graphs, sidebars, and extra features are not included.

Think and Share

1. Could this story happen in real life? Tell why or why not.

2. What happened at the beginning of the story? What happened in the middle? What happened at the end?

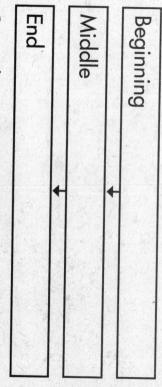

Beginning	→
Middle	→
End	→

3. On a sheet of paper, write three words from this book that have a short e sound. Use each word in a complete sentence.

4. Would you like to help with a project such as the one in the story? Tell why or why not.

A Wildlife Buffet

by Libby McCord

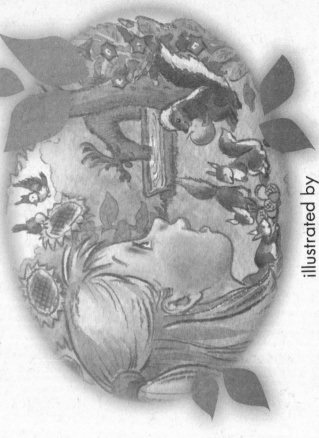

illustrated by
Aleksey Ivanov

PEARSON

Scott
Foresman

Editorial Offices: Glenview, Illinois • Parsippany, New Jersey • New York, New York
Sales Offices: Needham, Massachusetts • Duluth, Georgia • Glenview, Illinois
Coppell, Texas • Ontario, California • Mesa, Arizona

Habitats

A habitat is a place where plants and animals live. There are many different kinds of habitats. A forest is a habitat. An ocean is a habitat. A desert is a habitat. A swamp is a habitat too.

Habitats have what animals need to live. Habitats have air. Habitats have food for animals. Habitats have shelter for some animals.

This savanna is a habitat.

Every effort has been made to secure permission and provide appropriate credit for photographic material. The publisher deeply regrets any omission and pledges to correct errors called to its attention in subsequent editions.

Unless otherwise acknowledged, all photographs are the property of Scott Foresman, a division of Pearson Education.

Photo locators denoted as folllows: Top (T), Center (C), Bottom (B), Left (L), Right (R), Background (Bkgd)

Illustrations by Aleksey Ivanov

Photograph 12 Corbis

ISBN: 0-328-13156-3

Cary and her mom did go back. Cary couldn't believe what she saw. Hummingbirds drank from the morning glories. A mouse munched berries. Squirrels ate acorns. A deer drank water. A skunk ate apples. Many birds pecked at the sunflower seeds. The buffet was a big success!

11

Cary had been waiting for Saturday, and now it was here! This was the day she and her mom would be going to the Wildlife Shelter. They were going to help with a new project.

Cary and the group worked hard all day. They planted many kinds of plants. When they were finished, they all felt proud of their work.

"Come see us through the summer and fall," said Bev. "Then you can see the animals eating from the buffet!"

Cary thought she would burst with excitement! She loved animals. Now she was going to do something important to help them.

4

"We need to make sure the animals do not get used to any food they would not find in their natural habitat," explained Bev. "If they did, some birds might not fly south to find food. Some animals might not sleep in the winter. So we will only use plants that grow naturally."

9

"Maybe we can make strings of peanuts to feed the animals," said Cary.

"That is a good idea," said Bev. "But let me tell you about our plans." Bev brought out a large poster to show the group. "We're going to grow plants that the animals can use for food."

Cary and her mom went inside the Wildlife Shelter. They met a man who was feeding baby birds. "How old are they?" Cary asked.

"They are one day old. We saw these birds hatch yesterday," the man said.

6

Cary and her mom went to join a group of volunteers.

"Welcome, everyone," said Bev. "I am Bev. I work here at the Wildlife Shelter. I am going to get you started. Let me explain what we will be doing."

7

"Many animals are losing their habitats. Without trees to live in or food to eat in a habitat, the animals can't survive," Bev told them. "So we are setting up a natural buffet to feed them."

"It will be like a lunchroom line!" said Cary.

Life Science

Science

Science

Animals Around the World

by Linda B. Ross

Suggested levels for Guided Reading, DRA™, Lexile®, and Reading Recovery™ are provided in the Pearson Scott Foresman Leveling Guide.

Genre	Comprehension Skills and Strategy	Text Feature
Narrative nonfiction	• Cause and Effect • Main Idea • Monitor and Fix Up	• Captions

Scott Foresman Reading Street 1.1.6

PEARSON
Scott Foresman

scottforesman.com

ISBN 0-328-13159-8

9 780328 131594

90000

Vocabulary

desert

forest

world

Word count: 240

Think and Share

1. Walruses make holes in ice with their tusks. Copy the chart on your paper. Point to the top oval. Tell why walruses make these holes.

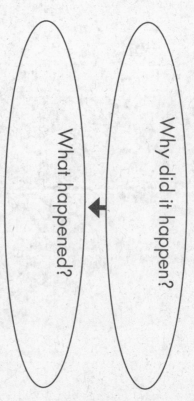

Why did it happen?

What happened?

2. Look back on page 8. What parts of page 8 help you understand more about the forest?

3. Find and tell which pages have the word *world* in them.

4. What did you learn from the caption on page 5?

Animals Around the World

by Linda B. Ross

PEARSON

Scott
Foresman

Editorial Offices: Glenview, Illinois • Parsippany, New Jersey • New York, New York
Sales Offices: Needham, Massachusetts • Duluth, Georgia • Glenview, Illinois
Coppell, Texas • Ontario, California • Mesa, Arizona

Every effort has been made to secure permission and provide appropriate credit for photographic material. The publisher deeply regrets any omission and pledges to correct errors called to its attention in subsequent editions.

Unless otherwise acknowledged, all photographs are the property of Scott Foresman, a division of Pearson Education.

Photo locators denoted as follows: Top (T), Center (C), Bottom (B), Left (L), Right (R), Background (Bkgd)

Opener: ©DK Images; 1 (T, Bkgd) ©DK Images, (T, C) Getty Images; 3 (T, C, B) Getty Images, (R, L) ©DK Images; 4 (T, B) Getty Images; 5 Getty Images; 6 ©DK Images; 7 (BR) Getty Images; 8 (T) Getty Images, (C) ©DK Images; 9 (TL, BR, C) ©DK Images; 9 (TR, BL) Getty Images; 10 (L) Getty Images, (C) ©DK Images; 11 ©DK Images

ISBN: 0-328-13159-8

Here's How to Do It!

1. Think about what you would ask one animal about living in its habitat.
2. Work together to write five questions and answers.
3. Practice the interview out loud.
4. Create costumes for each part.
5. Perform the interview for an audience.

11

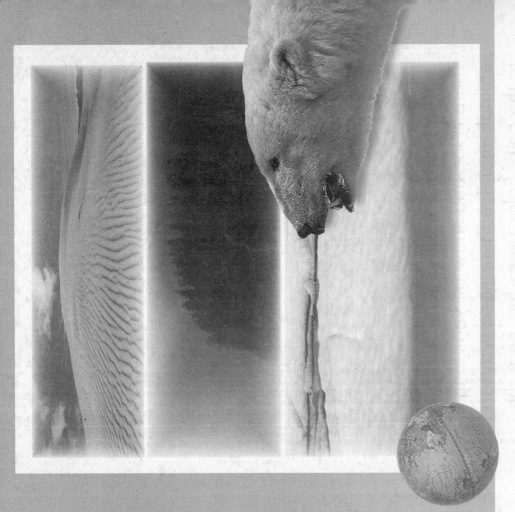

Many kinds of animals live around the world. Each animal lives in its own place. Keep reading to learn about some of these animals. You will find out about the places where they live.

Now Try This

Conduct an Interview

Suppose you could ask an animal what it is like to live where it lives. Work in pairs to create this kind of interview. One partner should be the interviewer. The interviewer will ask the questions. One partner will play the part of the animal. The animal will give answers.

The North Pole is a very cold place. There is ice and snow all year long. The animals that live there need ways to live in the cold. Polar bears live near the North Pole. Polar bears have thick fur. Their fur helps them stay warm.

These are just some of the different places around the world where animals live. Every animal has a place where it belongs. That place is its home.

Some animals live where it is cold.

Walruses live near the North Pole too. Walruses use their tusks to make holes in the sea ice. They swim to the hole to take a breath of air. They also use their tusks to grab the ice. This helps them crawl out of the water.

The forest is filled with animal life.

Forests are places where the weather can be hot or cold. Many animals make their homes in the forest. Toads live in forests. Toads sleep in mud holes or under rocks when it is cold.

Deserts are very dry. These places get very little rain. Animals that live in the desert need to be able to live with only a little water and food.

Camels live in the desert. Camels have humps that help them store food. They do not need to find food all the time.

Desert animals find ways to store food.

School Rules

by Bonita Ferraro

illustrated by Bettina Ogden

Suggested levels for Guided Reading, DRA,™ Lexile® and Reading Recovery™ are provided in the Pearson Scott Foresman Leveling Guide.

Genre	Comprehension Skills and Strategy
Animal fantasy	• Main Idea • Character • Predict

Scott Foresman Reading Street 1.2.1

PEARSON

Scott Foresman

scottforesman.com

ISBN 0-328-13162-8

9 780328 131624

90000

Vocabulary

chores

cooperation

household

rules

Word count: 365

Think and Share

1. What is *School Rules* all about? Draw this chart on your paper. Draw pictures in the boxes to show which parts of the story helped you understand it.

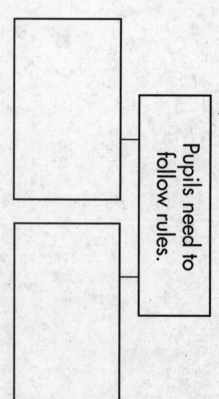

Pupils need to follow rules.

2. When Scamper spilled his drink, did you guess what Chip would say? How did you know?

3. If someone asked you what a rule is, how would you answer?

4. Why do you think Bunny, Scamper, and Chip broke the rules?

School Rules

by Bonita Ferraro

illustrated by Bettina Ogden

PEARSON
Scott
Foresman

Editorial Offices: Glenview, Illinois • Parsippany, New Jersey • New York, New York
Sales Offices: Needham, Massachusetts • Duluth, Georgia • Glenview, Illinois
Coppell, Texas • Ontario, California • Mesa, Arizona

Rules, Rules, Rules

Take a look around your school. Do you see any signs that have rules on them? How do you find out about school rules? Are some of the rules in your school the same as the rules in this story?

Every school has rules. In fact, there are rules every place you go. Rules are made to help people stay safe. They also help us to remember to be fair. Think about the rules in your life. How do they keep you safe? How do they help you remember to be fair?

12

Copyright © Pearson Education, Inc.

ISBN: 0-328-13162-8

Illustrations by Betina Ogden

Photo locators denoted as follows: Top (T), Center (C), Bottom (B), Left (L), Right (R), Background (Bkgd)

Unless otherwise acknowledged, all photographs are the property of Scott Foresman, a division of Pearson Education.

Every effort has been made to secure permission and provide appropriate credit for photographic material. The publisher deeply regrets any omission and pledges to correct errors called to its attention in subsequent editions.

2 3 4 5 6 7 8 9 10 V010 14 13 12 11 10 09 08 07 06 05

It was a long first day of school for the three best friends.

"Tomorrow we should try harder to follow the rules," said Bunny.

"You can count on us!" her friends shouted.

11

It was the first day of school for Bunny, Chip, and Scamper.

"We are like a big family. Our household is this school," Mrs. Pine said. "We all have chores to do. We all have rules to follow. Cooperation means working together. Can I count on your cooperation?"

Chores

1. Water the plants.
2. Erase the board.
3. Feed the fish.

"YIKES!" yelled Scamper as he jumped in surprise. Scamper's new white shirt had red juice all over it.

"I am so sorry, Scamper," said Chip. "I didn't follow the rule about no noise at lunch. I want to be fair. I'll help you try to wash out the stain."

Bunny, Chip, and Scamper nodded. Mrs. Pine could count on their cooperation. She could count on them to be good and to follow the rules.

School Rules
1. Walk, do not run, in the halls.
2. Take turns on the playground.
3. Eat quietly at lunchtime.

At lunch, Chip was finished eating first. He was bored. He started to play with his lunch bag.

"I am tired of waiting," Chip said to himself. He blew air into his lunch bag. Then he popped it as loudly as he could.

Later that morning, Bunny was on her way to the playground.

"I am late," Bunny said. "I need to hurry!" Bunny ran down the hall as fast as she could.

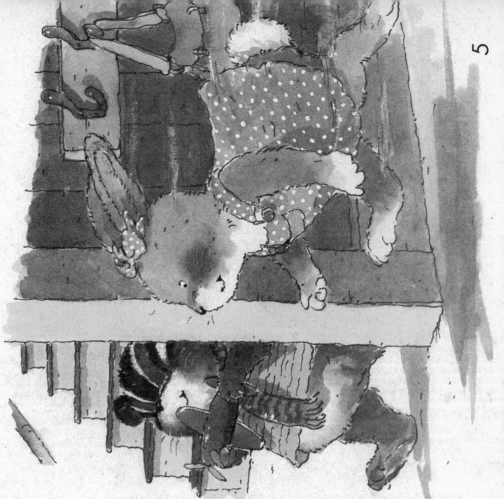

"HEY!" yelled Bunny as she watched Scamper get on the swing. "It is not your turn! It is my turn now!"

"I'm so sorry, Bunny," said Scamper. "I didn't follow the rule about waiting my turn. I want to be fair. I'll let you have your turn."

"WHOA!" yelled Chip as Bunny ran into him. Chip's clay plane fell. He couldn't catch it. It dropped on the floor and broke.

"I am so sorry, Chip," said Bunny. "I didn't follow the rule about walking. I want to be fair. I'll help put your plane back together."

6

During recess, Bunny was waiting her turn for the swing. Scamper was next in line.

"When will it be my turn? I want to be next," Scamper said to himself. Chip got off. Scamper grabbed the swing as hard as he could.

7

Social Studies

School:
Then and Now

by Marianne Lenihan

Scott Foresman Reading Street 1.2.2

Genre	Comprehension Skills and Strategy	Text Features
Expository nonfiction	• Cause and Effect • Draw Conclusions • Monitor and Fix Up	• Captions • Labels

PEARSON

Scott
Foresman

scottforesman.com

ISBN 0-328-13165-2

90000

9 780328 131655

Vocabulary

group
respect
share

Word count: 310

Think and Share

1. Many students of long ago did chores after school. Draw the chart on your own paper. Tell why they did chores.

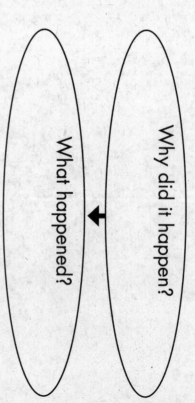

Why did it happen?

What happened?

2. Read page 6 again. If you didn't understand what a hornbook was like, how might the picture help you?

3. Make a list of words from the book that tell about school. Which words tell about your school? Which tell about schools long ago?

4. Looking at the pictures of schools of then and now, what differences can you see?

School:
Then and Now

by Marianne Lenihan

PEARSON
Scott
Foresman

Editorial Offices: Glenview, Illinois • Parsippany, New Jersey • New York, New York
Sales Offices: Needham, Massachusetts • Duluth, Georgia • Glenview, Illinois
Coppell, Texas • Ontario, California • Mesa, Arizona

Every effort has been made to secure permission and provide appropriate credit for photographic material. The publisher deeply regrets any omission and pledges to correct errors called to its attention in subsequent editions.

Unless otherwise acknowledged, all photographs are the property of Scott Foresman, a division of Pearson Education.

Photo locators denoted as follows: Top (T), Center (C), Bottom (B), Left (L), Right (R), Background (Bkgd)

Illustration by Amy Loeffler

Opener: (C, B) Getty Images; 1 Getty Images; 3 (C) Jonathan Lange/Library of Congress, (BR) Brand X Pictures; 4 (B) Library of Congress, (CR) Brand X Pictures; 5 Getty Images; 6 Getty Images; 7 (CL) Brand X Pictures, (B) Michael Newman/PhotoEdit; 8 John Vachon/Library of Congress; 9 (C) Getty Images, Bettmann/Corbis; 10 Getty Images; 11 Library of Congress

---

Copy this poem onto a piece of paper. Fill in the missing parts. Try to make a rhyme.

I Know a Girl

I know a girl named _____.

Her brothers are _____ and _____.

They laugh and play

They eat _____

And then they _____.

11

"Older children, please take out your hornbooks. Younger children, please recite your numbers."

If you were a student in the early days of the United States, that is how your school day might have started.

A school bell started many school days.

Now Try This

Practice Like a Student of Long Ago

Copy these activities onto a piece of paper. Suppose you are a student of long ago.

Fill in the missing letters and numbers.

Activity

A B ___ D E F G ___ J

K ___ M N O ___ ___ S

___ ___ V ___ Y ___

1 2 3 ___ ___ 6 7 ___ ___ 11

___ 14 ___ ___ 19 ___

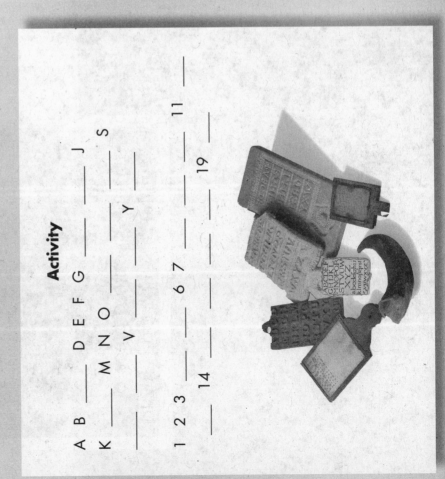

School was very different then. Not every child went to school. The children who went to school were all in the same room, no matter how old they were. They even shared the same teacher! The children sat in groups on wooden benches. They practiced reading and writing. They did math too.

4

Schools are very different today than they were a long time ago. But something very important happened in schools long ago, and it still happens in schools today—learning!

9

Today in the United States, all children must go to school. Children are in classrooms with other children who are about the same age.

Now children learn how to read and write and do math just like children in earlier times. Children today study many other subjects too. All school children are taught to respect others.

Sometimes students of the past had to go far to get to school. Many walked a long way. Today most students ride school buses or are driven in cars.

After school many children long ago had chores to do to help their families. Children today often have time to play when the school day is over.

A schoolhouse

Imagine schools with no books! Most students of long ago had only hornbooks. Hornbooks were not really books at all!

A hornbook looked like a wooden paddle. The alphabet and numbers were carved into one side. A sheet of paper was attached to the other side.

Most students today go to schools that are filled with things to help them learn and play. There are books and computers and maps. There are writing pads and pencils and crayons. There are playgrounds and gyms.

Social Studies

Mayor Mom

by Marianne Lenihan

Genre	Comprehension Skills and Strategy	Text Features
Narrative nonfiction	• Author's Purpose • Cause and Effect • Ask Questions	• Time Designations

Scott Foresman Reading Street 1.2.3

PEARSON

Scott
Foresman

scottforesman.com

ISBN 0-328-13168-7

9 780328 131686

90000

Vocabulary

citizen

community

law

leader

Word count: 315

Think and Share

1. Why do you think the author started with the beginning of the mayor's day?

2. If you could meet Mayor Martinez, what questions would you ask her? Copy the chart on your paper. Fill it out. Write your question in the W box.

What We **K**now	What We **W**ant to Know	What We **L**earned

3. Mayor Martinez talked with the school children about how a law is made. What is a law?

4. What do the clock pictures throughout the book tell you about the mayor's day?

Mayor Mom

by Marianne Lenihan

Editorial Offices: Glenview, Illinois • Parsippany, New Jersey • New York, New York
Sales Offices: Needham, Massachusetts • Duluth, Georgia • Glenview, Illinois
Coppell, Texas • Ontario, California • Mesa, Arizona

Every effort has been made to secure permission and provide appropriate credit for photographic material. The publisher deeply regrets any omission and pledges to correct errors called to its attention in subsequent editions.

Unless otherwise acknowledged, all photographs are the property of Scott Foresman, a division of Pearson Education.

Photo locators denoted as follows: Top (T), Center (C), Bottom (B), Left (L), Right (R), Background (Bkgd)

Opener: (C) Getty Images, (B) DK Images; 1 Getty Images; 3 DK Images; 4 (C) DK Images, (B) Getty Images; 5 Getty Images; 6 DK Images; 7 Getty Images; 8 (B, C) Getty Images; 9 DK Images; 10 Getty Images

ISBN: 0-328-13168-7

2 3 4 5 6 7 8 9 10 V010 14 13 12 11 10 09 08 07 06 05

Here's How to Do It!

Copy this planner onto a piece of paper and plan out your day as mayor.

Today's date is _____ .

This is what my schedule is today:

9 o'clock
_____

11 o'clock Talk to a first-grade class.
_____

1 o'clock
_____

3 o'clock
_____

5 o'clock
_____

11

Dear Carlos,

My mom is the new mayor of our town! I'm sending you pictures, and I want to tell you about her job.

Here's my mom at work. Her day at the office starts at eight o'clock.

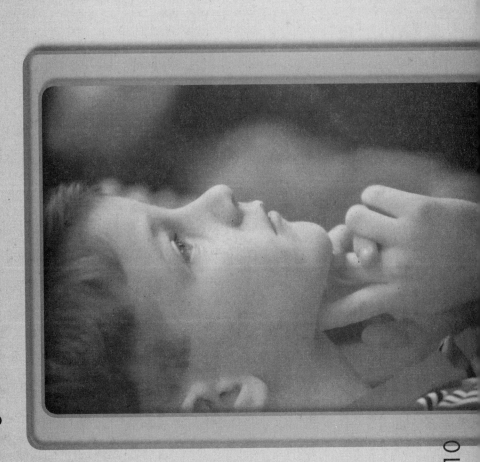

Now Try This

Be Mayor for a Day!

If you were the mayor of your town or city for a day, what kinds of things would you do? You might do some of the same things Mayor Martinez does. You might do different things too.

Mom has many things to do every day. She checks her schedule each morning when she gets to work. These are some of the people she will meet with this week. Mom works hard at her job.

At four o'clock, Mom is still busy at work. Everyone says she is a good leader. I think she is an even better mom. I hope you like all the pictures. Write back soon!

Your friend,
Ramon Martinez

One of my mom's first meetings is at nine o'clock in the community center. Here is a picture of it. She says people want to decide the best way to use the community center. I think they need to have more activities there for kids!

This picture is from last year's festival. Remember how much fun we had? The people in the picture are some of the business owners who want to help organize this year's festival. I hope you can come to the festival again this year.

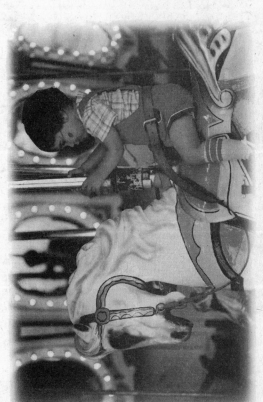

Here's the new playground. A boy sent a letter to Mom asking for an empty lot to be turned into a place where kids can play. Mom met with community leaders. They decided that a new playground was a good idea. Mom says the boy is a good citizen because he cares about his community.

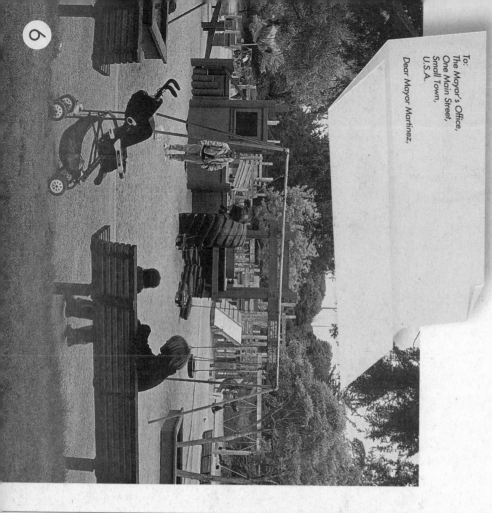

To:
The Mayor's Office,
One Main Street,
Small Town,
U.S.A.

Dear Mayor Martinez,

Here is a picture of me at school having lunch. Mom came to our school to talk about her job. She told us how a law is made. We asked a lot of questions. When I asked her a question, I remembered to call her Mayor Martinez and not Mom! She even ate lunch with my class that day.

Life Science

Science

Dinosaur Detectives

by Beth Lewis

Genre	Comprehension Skills and Strategy	Text Features
Expository nonfiction	• Sequence • Draw Conclusions • Monitor and Fix Up	• Captions • Labels

Scott Foresman Reading Street 1.2.4

PEARSON
Scott Foresman

scottforesman.com

ISBN 0-328-13171-7

9 780328 131716

90000

Vocabulary

enemy
extinct
protect

Word count: 328

Note: The total word count includes words in the running text and headings only. Numerals and words in chapter titles, captions, labels, diagrams, charts, graphs, sidebars, and extra features are not included.

Think and Share

1. What dinosaurs did you read about in this book? Copy the chart on your paper. Write the names of the dinosaurs in the order you read about them.

1. First	
2. Next	←
3. Then	←
4. Last	←

2. What were some ways the triceratops protected itself? Reread page 7 to check your answer.

3. What does the word extinct mean? Use it in a complete sentence.

4. Look at the picture of the allosaurus on page 8. What parts are labeled? What parts are not labeled?

Dinosaur Detectives

by Beth Lewis

Editorial Offices: Glenview, Illinois • Parsippany, New Jersey • New York, New York
Sales Offices: Needham, Massachusetts • Duluth, Georgia • Glenview, Illinois
Coppell, Texas • Ontario, California • Mesa, Arizona

Every effort has been made to secure permission and provide appropriate credit for photographic material. The publisher deeply regrets any omission and pledges to correct errors called to its attention in subsequent editions.

Unless otherwise acknowledged, all photographs are the property of Scott Foresman, a division of Pearson Education.

Photo locators denoted as follows: Top (T), Center (C), Bottom (B), Left (L), Right (R), Background (Bkgd)

All photos belong to DK Images.

ISBN: 0-328-13171-7

2 3 4 5 6 7 8 9 10 V010 14 13 12 11 10 09 08 07 06 05

Here's How to Do It!

1. Find out about a dinosaur. It can be one you read about in this book or another one. Use a book, a magazine article, or even a Web site.

2. Write the name of the dinosaur you read about at the top of a large sheet of drawing paper.

3. Draw a picture of the dinosaur. Be sure to include as many details as you can.

4. Label the parts of the dinosaur, such as the head, neck, claws, teeth, legs, and tail. Draw a line to each part and write the word or words that tell about the part.

5. Share your dinosaur diagram with the class. Point to and name the dinosaur parts you labeled.

11

Dinosaurs were animals that lived millions of years ago. Then they became extinct. This means they don't exist anymore. To find out about dinosaurs, we need to become dinosaur detectives. We need to find fossils. A fossil is a part or a print of a plant or animal that lived a long time ago.

These are allosaurus fossils.

Now Try This

Become a Dinosaur Detective

You can be a dinosaur detective even if you can't search for fossils. Instead, you can search for information about dinosaurs in books, in magazines, and on the Internet.

Apatosaurus
Head
Neck
Tail
Legs

Some fossils show that dinosaurs had ways to stay safe. They had to protect themselves from other dinosaurs, or maybe other kinds of animals. We can look at fossils to see how each kind of dinosaur might have protected itself from an enemy.

This is a fossil of an apatosaurus's claw.

These are just some of the things fossils have told us about dinosaurs. There is so much more to learn. When we put fossil clues together, we'll be dinosaur detectives. If you keep learning about dinosaurs, you can be a dinosaur detective too!

This is a fossil of dinosaur footprints.

The stegosaurus had a row of bones running down its back. It also had sharp spikes on its long tail. It protected itself by swinging its tail back and forth. It may also have used the bony plates on its back to stay safe.

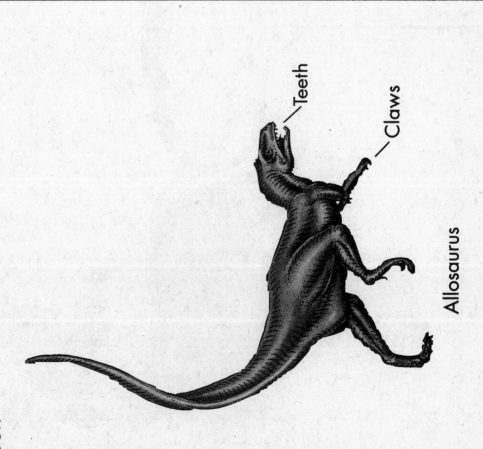

Spikes

Bony plates

Stegosaurus

Scientists think the allosaurus hunted many plant-eating dinosaurs. These hunters also needed ways to stay safe. The allosaurus had a large jaw and long, sharp teeth. That might have been enough to protect the allosaurus. But it also had three sharp claws on each front foot!

Teeth

Claws

Allosaurus

The apatosaurus was very big. We think it was so big that it needed to spend most of its time eating! Its size might have been enough to keep it safe. But the apatosaurus also might have used its tail to help fight off its enemies.

Tail

Apatosaurus

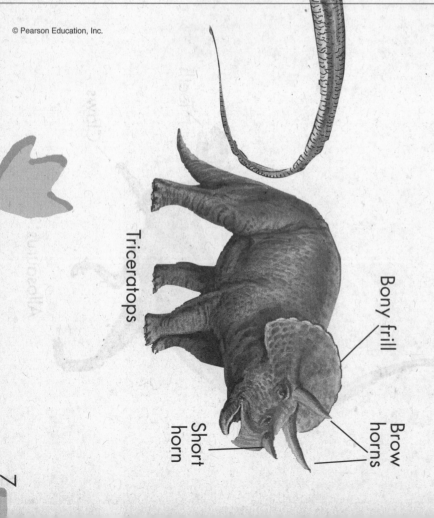

The triceratops had many ways to protect itself. It was a very big dinosaur. It probably lived and traveled in a herd. It might have been easier to stay safe in this group. The triceratops had three large horns. It had bones on its neck and shoulders. These things protected the triceratops.

Bony frill

Brow horns

Short horn

Triceratops

Suggested levels for Guided Reading, DRA,™ Lexile,® and Reading Recovery™ are provided in the Pearson Scott Foresman Leveling Guide.

Science

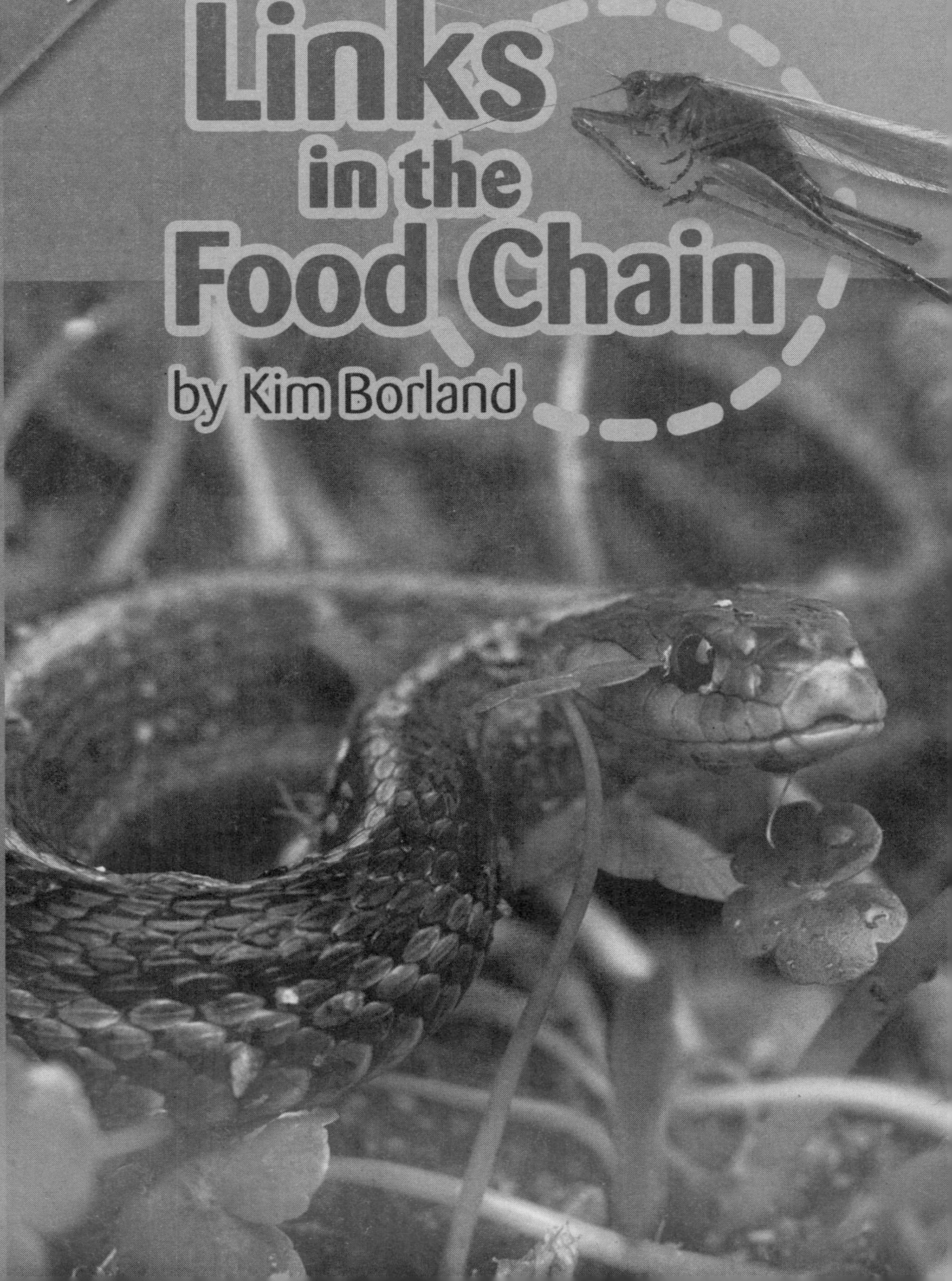

Genre	Comprehension Skills and Strategy	Text Features
Expository nonfiction	• Author's Purpose • Cause and Effect • Preview	• Labels • Diagrams

Scott Foresman Reading Street 1.2.5

PEARSON
Scott Foresman
scottforesman.com

ISBN 0-328-13174-1
9 780328 131747 90000

Science

Life Science

Links in the Food Chain

by Kim Borland

Vocabulary

environment

require

thrive

Word count: 284

Note: The total word count includes words in the running text and headings only. Numerals and words in chapter titles, captions, labels, diagrams, charts, graphs, sidebars, and extra features are not included.

Think and Share

1. Why did the writer tell about the food chain before she talked about what could happen if the food chain changes?

2. What did you do to get ready to read this book? Did it help you understand it better?

3. Page 8 says, "The grass might thrive." What other words can you think of that mean the same as *thrive*?

4. How is the diagram on page 8 the same as the diagram on pages 6 and 7? How is it different? What does this difference tell you about the food chain? Fill in a chart like this one.

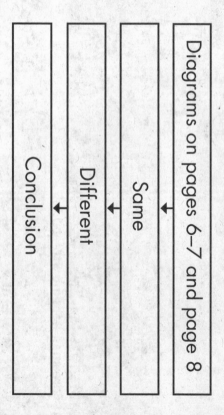

Diagrams on pages 6–7 and page 8
Same
Different
Conclusion

Links in the Food Chain

by Kim Borland

Editorial Offices: Glenview, Illinois • Parsippany, New Jersey • New York, New York
Sales Offices: Needham, Massachusetts • Duluth, Georgia • Glenview, Illinois
Coppell, Texas • Ontario, California • Mesa, Arizona

Every effort has been made to secure permission and provide appropriate credit for photographic material. The publisher deeply regrets any omission and pledges to correct errors called to its attention in subsequent editions.

Unless otherwise acknowledged, all photographs are the property of Scott Foresman, a division of Pearson Education.

Photo locators denoted as follows: Top (T), Center (C), Bottom (B), Left (L), Right (R), Background (Bkgd)

Opener: (T) Brand X Pictures, (C) Getty Images; 1 (TR) Brand X Pictures, (CL) Getty Images; 3 (TL, TC, CR, BR) Getty Images, (BL) Digital Vision; 4 (L, R) Digital Vision; 5 Digital Vision; 6 (TL) Getty Images, (BR) Digital Vision; 7 Getty Images; 8 (CR, TL) Getty Images, (BC) Digital Vision; 9 Digital Vision; 11 Getty Images

ISBN: 0-328-13174-1

2 3 4 5 6 7 8 9 10 V010 14 13 12 11 10 09 08 07 06 05

Here's How to Do It!

1. Find a large sheet of white construction paper. Get some crayons too.
2. Write *Living Things* across the top of your paper.
3. Draw pictures of plants and animals that you know about. (Hint: They can be plants and animals that live on land or in water!)
4. Write the name of each plant or animal under its picture.
5. Share your drawings with your class.

Living things are everywhere! Plants are living things. Animals are living things. You are a living thing too.

Living things require food. Food gives living things the energy they need to live and grow.

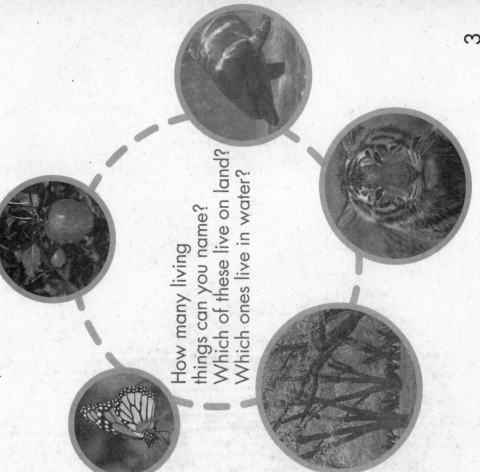

How many living things can you name? Which of these live on land? Which ones live in water?

Now Try This

Living Things Poster

You know that living things are all around. Now it's your turn to share what you know about these living things!

Many living things eat other living things. This makes a food chain. Each living thing is a link in the food chain.

Food chains are found in every environment. They are all alike in one important way. Food chains begin with the sun and plants.

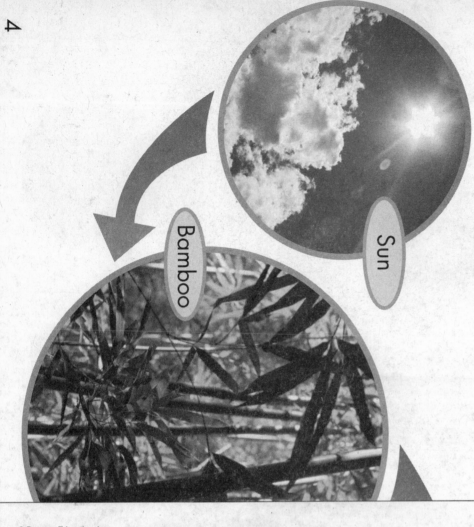

Sun

Bamboo

4

Food is a requirement of most living things. All living things are linked to other living things in food chains. As living things eat and are eaten, food chains go on. Food chains can change as environments change.

9

Did you know that most plants make their own food? It's true! They use the energy of the sun to make their food. When an animal eats the plant's leaves, the sun's energy is passed on. The sun's energy goes to the plant and then to the animal.

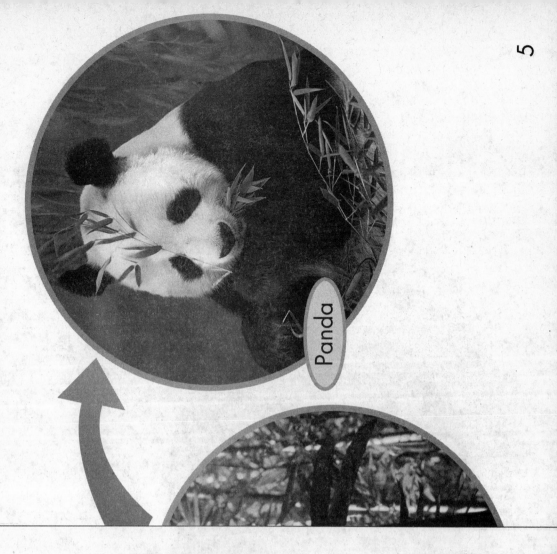

Panda

A change in one part of the food chain causes a change in the other parts. What if there were no more grasshoppers?

The grasshoppers would not eat the grass. The grass might thrive, but the snakes would not have food. They could die if there was not enough to eat.

Let's take a close look at a forest. In a forest there are many food chains. The plants and animals can be part of more than one food chain. The plants and animals need each other to live.

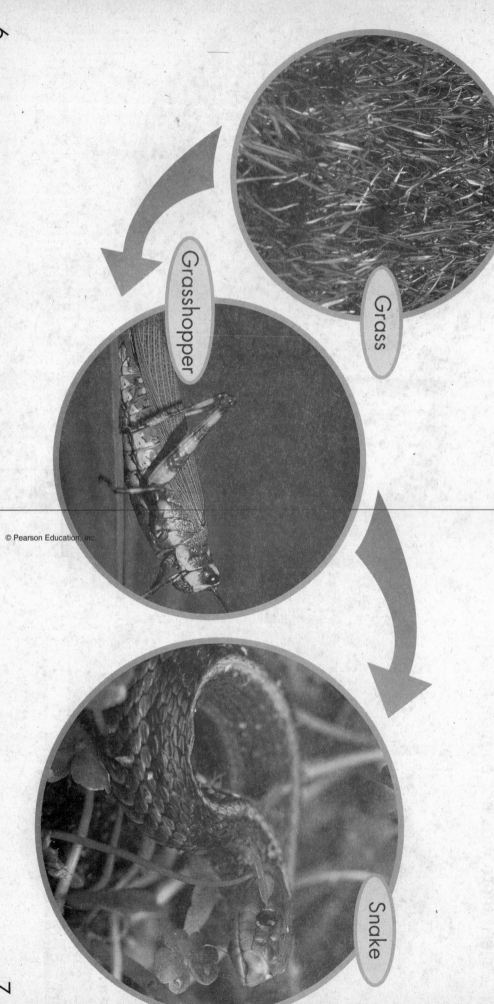

Grass

Grasshopper

Snake

© Pearson Education, Inc.

Some grasshoppers eat grass. A snake eats grasshoppers. The grass, the grasshopper, and the snake are linked. They form a food chain. Each plant and animal is a link in that chain.

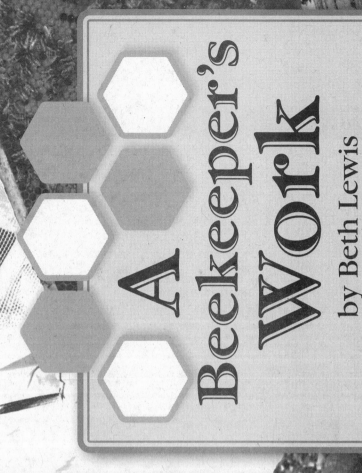

A Beekeeper's Work

by Beth Lewis

Social Studies

Genre	Comprehension Skills and Strategy	Text Feature
Expository nonfiction	• Compare and Contrast • Main Idea • Preview	• Captions

Scott Foresman Reading Street 1.2.6

ISBN 0-328-13177-6

9 780328 131778

90000

PEARSON

Scott Foresman

scottforesman.com

Vocabulary

individual

industrious

special

Word count: 304

Think and Share

1. How are worker bees and queen bees alike? How are they different? Use a diagram like this to write your answer.

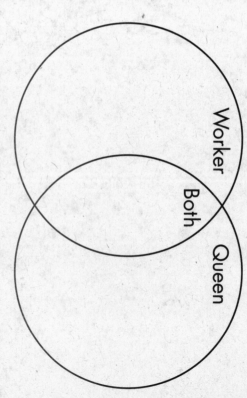

Worker   Both   Queen

2. What did you want to find out from reading *A Beekeeper's Work*? What did you do when you didn't understand something you read?

3. Make a list of words from the book and other words you know that have the long e sound spelled ee.

4. A caption helps the reader understand a picture on the page of a book. What information did you learn from the caption on page 6?

A Beekeeper's Work

by Beth Lewis

Editorial Offices: Glenview, Illinois • Parsippany, New Jersey • New York, New York
Sales Offices: Needham, Massachusetts • Duluth, Georgia • Glenview, Illinois
Coppell, Texas • Ontario, California • Mesa, Arizona

ISBN: 0-328-13177-6

Here's How to Do It!

1. Look in books, magazines, and on the Internet to find out about beekeeping suits.

2. Make a copy of a picture of a beekeeping outfit. You can use the one on page 5 of this book or another one that you find.

3. Use a dark marker to draw lines to each part of the outfit. Write the name of the part next to each line.

4. Share your diagram with the class.

Beekeeping Outfit

11

Many people don't like to be around bees. They are afraid they might get stung. But that's not true for a beekeeper. A beekeeper chooses to be around bees. Read on to find out more about a beekeeper's work!

Now Try This

Label the Parts

What parts of a beekeeper's outfit help him or her stay safe? What are these parts called? Look for the answers to these questions. Then draw a diagram of a beekeeping suit to show what you have learned.

Beekeepers use special hives that are made out of wood. Their hives are made of boxes that open at the top and bottom. Inside each box, the bees build their honeycombs on wooden frames that move.

A beekeeper's beehives

4

Some beekeepers sell honey and wax to factories. The factories then make goods with the honey and wax.

People use honey. Beeswax is made into candles, crayons, shoe polish, lipstick, and many other products. Many things we use every day start with bees and beekeepers!

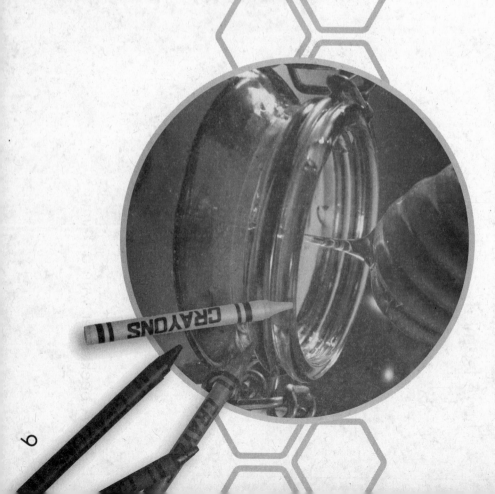

9

A beekeeper uses a tool called a smoker to spray smoke on the bees. The smoke helps keep the bees from stinging. This helps keep the beekeeper safe. The beekeeper checks for eggs and young bees. He or she gives the bees sugar syrup if they need food. The beekeeper may also give them medicine.

Beekeepers wear special outfits that protect them from being stung.

In late summer or fall, beekeepers take the frames from the hives to collect the honeycombs. Next, they put the honeycombs in a machine. The machine spins the honey and separates it from the comb. Then the combs are melted down to make wax.

A beekeeper with a frame

Bees that live in a hive built by a beekeeper are like bees that live in the wild. Most of them are worker bees. These industrious, hard-working bees do many jobs. Some worker bees collect nectar and pollen from the flowers. Other worker bees store pollen, make honey, and clean the hive.

Bees live in a large group called a colony. A colony of bees lives in a hive.

There is one individual queen bee in each hive. She is the only bee that lays eggs. There are also drones. Drones do not work and cannot sting. They help the queen bee.

Bees live in a large group called a colony. A colony of bees lives in a hive.

Life Science

Your Amazing Body!

by Lana Rios

illustrated by CD Hullinger

Genre	Comprehension Skills and Strategy	Text Feature
Expository nonfiction	• Compare and Contrast • Author's Purpose • Predict	• Captions

Scott Foresman Reading Street 1.3.1

ISBN 0-328-13180-6

9 780328 131808

90000

PEARSON

Scott Foresman

scottforesman.com

Think and Share

1. How are a two-year-old child's teeth different from an adult's teeth? How are they the same? Use a diagram like the one below to write your answers.

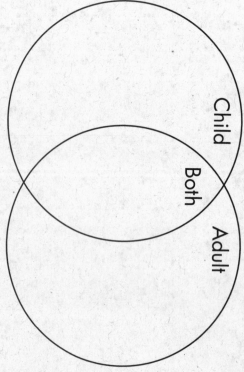

Child   Both   Adult

2. How tall do you think you will be when you are an adult? Why do you think that is true?

3. Find and write the three words on page 3 that have a y at the end that makes the long e sound.

4. A caption explains a picture and gives readers information. What information did you learn from the caption on page 5?

Vocabulary

adult
healthy
measurement

Word count: 293

Note: The total word count includes words in the running text and headings only. Numerals and words in chapter titles, captions, labels, diagrams, charts, graphs, sidebars, and extra features are not included.

Your Amazing Body!

by Lana Rios

illustrated by CD Hullinger

Editorial Offices: Glenview, Illinois • Parsippany, New Jersey • New York, New York
Sales Offices: Needham, Massachusetts • Duluth, Georgia • Glenview, Illinois
Coppell, Texas • Ontario, California • Mesa, Arizona

Every effort has been made to secure permission and provide appropriate credit for photographic material. The publisher deeply regrets any omission and pledges to correct errors called to its attention in subsequent editions.

Unless otherwise acknowledged, all photographs are the property of Scott Foresman, a division of Pearson Education.

Photo locators denoted as follows: Top (T), Center (C), Bottom (B), Left (L), Right (R), Background (Bkgd)

Illustrations by CD Hullinger

ISBN: 0-328-13180-6

2 3 4 5 6 7 8 9 10 V010 14 13 12 11 10 09 08 07 06 05

Here's How to Do It!

1. On the pages draw pictures of: something you did when you were a baby; something you can do now; something you want to do when you are nine years old; something you want to do when you are an adult.

2. Write a sentence about each picture.

3. Make a cover for your book. Write a title on the cover, such as "I Grow and Change." Decorate your cover and write your name on it.

4. Staple your pages together to make a book.

5. Share your book with the class. You can continue to add pages to your book as you think of new ideas.

11

You have an amazing body! Just think about it. There was a lot you couldn't do when you were a baby. But now you can do so many things! Let's take a look at how your amazing body grows.

Now Try This

Growing and Changing Book

Make a book that shows how you grow and change. Each page can have a picture that shows something about you that is different now than it was when you were a baby.

Your bones hold you up. They give your body its shape. Without them, you would fall over like a floppy doll! They also protect the inside of your body. Your bones get bigger as you grow.

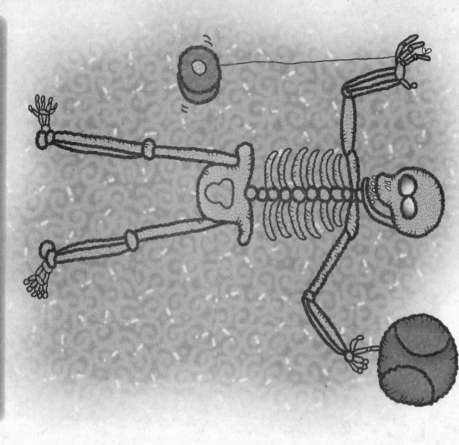

Bones are hard and strong. They protect the softer parts inside you.

Your heart pumps your blood. Did you know that your heart grows as you grow? Make a fist with your hand. No matter what size you are, your heart is a little bigger than your fist.

HEART

Now you know some of the ways your amazing body grows. You may not feel it, but you are growing right now!

When you were born, you had about 350 bones. As you get older, many of your bones will grow together to form larger bones. You will end up with about 206 bones when you become an adult.

The longest bone in your body is your thighbone.

Baby teeth begin to fall out when you are about six years old. Then your adult teeth grow in. Take good care of them. That way they will be healthy for the rest of your life! An adult has a full set of thirty-two teeth.

You need healthy teeth and gums to chew your food.

How tall will you be as an adult? That will depend on how tall the people in your family are. It will also depend on the food you eat.

Do you know how tall you are now? When you go to the doctor for a check-up, she takes your height measurement.

As you get older your teeth grow and change. You had no teeth at all when you were born. When you were about six months old, your first teeth began to show. These were your baby teeth. When you were two years old, you had about twenty baby teeth.

Baby teeth are also called milk teeth.

A Bed for Paul

by Ruth Renolo

illustrated by Al Lorenz

Suggested levels for Guided Reading, DRA™, Lexile® and Reading Recovery™ are provided in the Pearson Scott Foresman Leveling Guide.

Genre	Comprehension Skills and Strategy
Tall tale	• Plot • Character • Summarize

Scott Foresman Reading Street 1.3.2

PEARSON
Scott Foresman

scottforesman.com

Vocabulary

attempt

event

time line

Word count: 606

Think and Share

1. What does Paul do at the end of the book?

2. Think about what happened in the story. Write the chart on your paper and tell what happened.

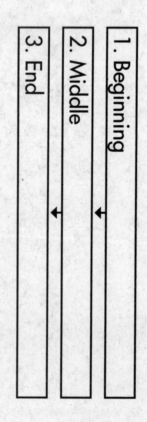

| 1. Beginning |
| 2. Middle |
| 3. End |

3. Look at the time line on pages 14 and 15. Tell what a time line is and describe what it shows in this book.

4. Paul's parents built a ship bed to solve their problem. Can you think of anything else they could have done? What would you do to solve this problem?

A Bed for Paul

by Ruth Renolo

illustrated by Al Lorenz

PEARSON

Scott
Foresman

Editorial Offices: Glenview, Illinois • Parsippany, New Jersey • New York, New York
Sales Offices: Needham, Massachusetts • Duluth, Georgia • Glenview, Illinois
Coppell, Texas • Ontario, California • Mesa, Arizona

Then and Now

Real lumberjacks had to be big and strong. But they weren't giants like Paul Bunyan. They had to cut down trees using tools to help them. They often rolled the tree trunks into fast running rivers to float them down to mills. Sometimes the heavy logs were pulled out of the woods and to the mills by teams of horses or oxen.

Lumberjacks today still cut and move logs to mills. But most of the time they use machines such as hand-held chainsaws, huge clippers, and claws on giant-sized wheels to help them cut. Then they use big, heavy cranes, lifters, and trucks to move the logs out of the woods.

16

Copyright © Pearson Education, Inc.

ISBN: 0-328-13183-0

Photographs 16 Corbis Media

Illustrations by Albert Lorenz

Photo locators denoted as follows: Top (T), Center (C), Bottom (B), Left (L), Right (R),
Background (Bkgd)

Unless otherwise acknowledged, all photographs are the property of Scott Foresman,
a division of Pearson Education.

Every effort has been made to secure permission and provide appropriate credit for
photographic material. The publisher deeply regrets any omission and pledges to
correct errors called to its attention in subsequent editions.

2 3 4 5 6 7 8 9 10 V010 14 13 12 11 10 09 08 07 06 05

© Pearson Education, Inc.

2 years old   16 years old

He lived in his cabin until he grew too
large once again. He knew it was time
to head out to find space to live.

Paul packed a sack made from a sail
and waved good-bye. He headed for
deep woods and wide country. He lived
happily ever after as the strongest and
biggest make-believe lumberjack of all!

15

When people need wood, they cut down the trees. People who cut down trees for a living are called lumberjacks. Long ago, as lumberjacks worked, they made up tall tales. Many of these tales were about Paul Bunyan. He was the biggest and strongest make-believe lumberjack of all!

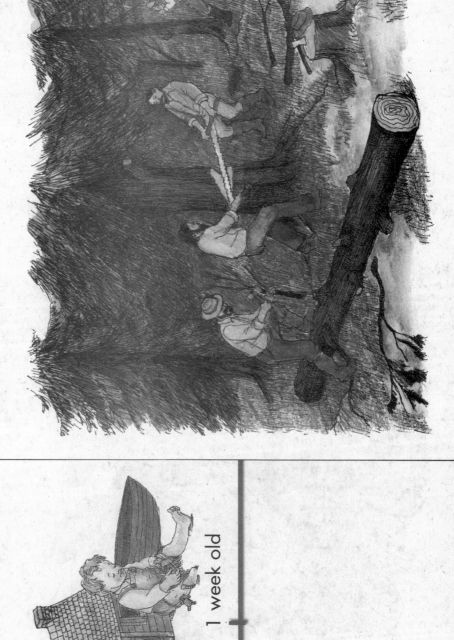

Now Paul was nearly as tall as the tallest pine tree in the woods. He knew it was up to him to find his own bed. Paul set off to gather wood to build the biggest log cabin and the biggest bed in all the land.

Paul Grows

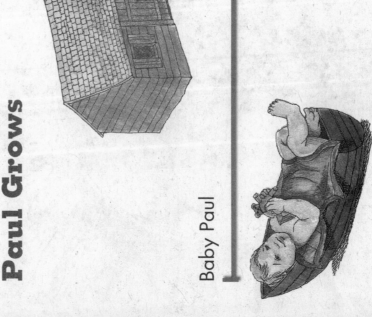

Baby Paul   1 week old

Most stories about Paul Bunyan were about his grown-up life. But some of the tales start with Paul as a baby. And what an amazing baby he was, or so the story goes!

Paul was way too big for a baby bed. He was even too big for his parents' bed. Paul was a huge baby!

The splash made all the water fly out of the lake! The ducks and fish were stunned to suddenly be on dry land. Paul quickly scooped the water into his huge hands and refilled the lake. Then he carefully put all the ducks and fish back into it.

As time passed, Paul's ship beds and quilts kept getting bigger. When he was sixteen, his ship bed was as big as the whole lake.

One morning, Paul stretched. His enormous body broke his ship bed! Boards flew and Paul fell into the lake with a mighty splash.

"What will we do?" Paul's mother moaned. A neighbor pulled a rowboat up to the Bunyans' cabin. The boat made a fine bed for Paul. But by the end of a week, Paul had grown as big as a moose.

"What bed will be big enough?" his father asked.

Paul's parents decided to build a bed the shape and size of a sailing ship. They thought this would be big enough for their gigantic son. By then, Paul had grown as big as the family cabin. Again, the neighbors came to help.

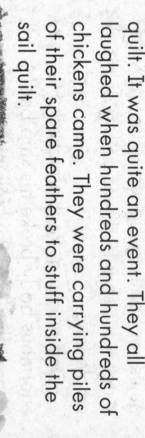

Everyone worked hard on Paul's quilt. It was quite an event. They all laughed when hundreds and hundreds of chickens came. They were carrying piles of their spare feathers to stuff inside the sail quilt.

When the ship bed was finished, they all knew it would not fit inside the cabin. So they pushed Paul's bed down to the lake and floated it on the water. They dropped an anchor so it would not float away. Then they all followed Paul as he toddled down to his new bed.

Again, neighbors came from miles around to help the Bunyans and their huge son. They all thought and thought about the problem. Then someone suggested they could sew together sails from ships to make a big enough quilt.

It was a snug fit, but Paul used his ship bed all summer long. When summer turned to fall, there was a new problem. They had already used every blanket they had to cover Paul. But this was not enough!

Paul was too big to fit in a cabin, where he could sleep by a warm fire. Paul's parents knew they had to find a way to keep him warm on the lake. "We must attempt to make a huge blanket," they decided.

Pins in the Map

by Nancy Day

illustrated by George Hamblin

Suggested levels for Guided Reading, DRA,™
Lexile,® and Reading Recovery™ are provided
in the Pearson Scott Foresman Leveling Guide.

Genre	Comprehension Skills and Strategy	
Realistic fiction	• Theme • Setting • Monitor and Fix Up	

Scott Foresman Reading Street 1.3.3

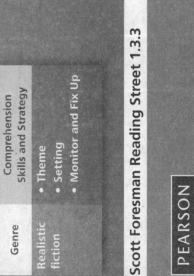

PEARSON

Scott
Foresman

scottforesman.com

ISBN 0-328-13186-5

9 780328 131860

90000

Vocabulary

arrive

depart

location

route

Word count: 566

Think and Share

1. What is the big idea of *Pins in the Map?*

2. On page 9 Katie said, "All the way across the country to Pacifica, California." How did the map help you understand what she meant?

3. Find the word relocate in this story. Say a complete sentence using this word.

4. Make a web of the different places Katie lived. Would you like to live in any of those places? Why or why not?

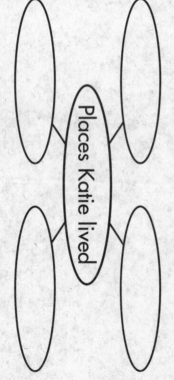

Places Katie lived

Pins in the Map

by Nancy Day
illustrated by George Hamblin

PEARSON
Scott Foresman

Editorial Offices: Glenview, Illinois • Parsippany, New Jersey • New York, New York
Sales Offices: Needham, Massachusetts • Duluth, Georgia • Glenview, Illinois
Coppell, Texas • Ontario, California • Mesa, Arizona

On the Move

Millions of Americans move each year. There are almost as many reasons to relocate as there are people who move! Sometimes people relocate for better jobs. Some move to be closer to family members. Others want to live in a different kind of place. It can be exciting to move to a new place!

16

Every effort has been made to secure permission and provide appropriate credit for photographic material. The publisher deeply regrets any omission and pledges to correct errors called to its attention in subsequent editions.

Unless otherwise acknowledged, all photographs are the property of Scott Foresman, a division of Pearson Education.

Photo locators denoted as follows: Top (T), Center (C), Bottom (B), Left (L), Right (R), Background (Bkgd)

Illustrations by George Hamblin

Photograph 16 Jose Luis Pelaez, Inc./Corbis

ISBN: 0-328-13186-5

2 3 4 5 6 7 8 9 10 V010 14 13 12 11 10 09 08 07 06 05

"I didn't want to move away from my friends and the mountains," Sam said. "But now I think I'm going to like living here." Sam pulled his pin out of Santa Fe and handed it to Katie.

Katie stuck the pin into Grand Haven.

© Pearson Education, Inc.

"Here, Boots," Katie called outside her family's cottage. Her cat didn't come to her.

"I hope he's not in the motel," Katie thought to herself. She went into the motel's lobby.

"Do you like living in this town?" Sam asked, his voice a little unsure.

"I do!" said Katie. "I like it more than anywhere else. Everybody knows everybody else. People are nice and friendly."

"Like you," Sam said.

Katie smiled. "It's fun meeting new people at the motel."

Boots was sitting on a boy's lap.
"Boots!" Katie scolded. "You're not
supposed to bother guests."
"I'm Sam," the boy smiled. "Boots
isn't bothering me at all. He looks like
my cat at home—wherever that is."
Sam's mouth turned down.

"So you moved again," Sam said.
"Yes," Katie answered. "My parents
sold the farm and bought this motel. It
wasn't such a long car trip to get here.
And here I get to see Lake Michigan."

"I'm Katie. Are you visiting? Where do you live?" Katie asked.

"I live here at your motel until my parents find a house," Sam replied. "My mom will be working here in Grand Haven, so we have to relocate. We used to live in Santa Fe, New Mexico."

Sam asked, "What did you do in Branchville?"

"I spent days watching my parents work on the old farmhouse. Sometimes I helped sell peaches at our stand. I'll never forget the smell of ripe peaches, and how the juice runs down your chin when you eat one," Katie smiled.

"I know about relocating. I have moved from one location to another my whole life," Katie said, pointing to a big map of the United States on the wall. "I've put pins in the spots where I've lived. Our motel guests stick in pins too."

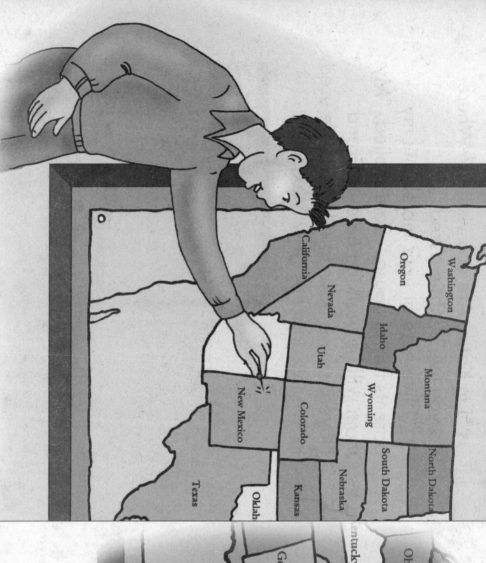

"Next, we moved to Branchville, South Carolina," said Katie. "My parents ran a peach farm there. It wasn't so bad taking the long route to get there. My brother could play games by that time!" Katie chuckled.

Sam placed a pin in Santa Fe. "First, we lived in New York City," Katie pointed. "We lived in a tiny apartment in a really tall building."

"What do you remember most about living there?" asked Sam.

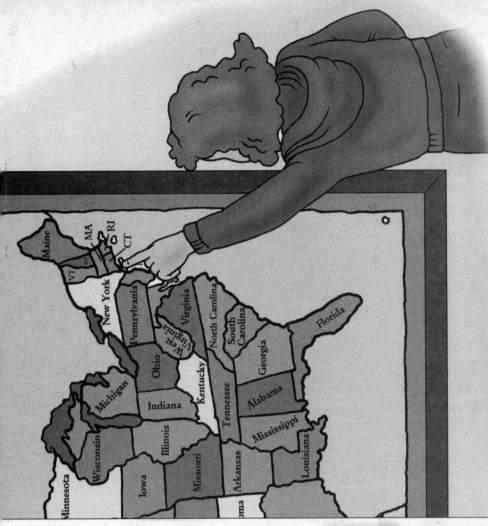

"It was great when we got there," Katie went on. "I could see the ocean from my bedroom window!"

"It was nice," Katie said. "The only trouble was that our house was the same shape as every other house! I could tell which one was ours only by the color and the gnome in the front yard."

"My dad worked in a big hotel. I remember watching people going in and out of the spinning door when I visited him at work. It was fun to watch all the people!" Katie laughed. "Then Dad got a job with a different hotel."

"Where did you move then?" Sam asked.

"All the way across the country to Pacifica, California." Katie showed him the pin. "It's near San Francisco. We packed our car. We drove for five days. My brother was too young to play any games with me. He cried all the way!"

8

9

The Mile-a-Minute Vine

by Nancy Day • illustrated by Victor Kennedy

Genre	Comprehension Skills and Strategy
Fantasy	• Plot • Main Idea • Visualize

Scott Foresman Reading Street 1.3.4

ISBN 0-328-13189-X

9 780328 131891

90000

PEARSON

Scott Foresman

scottforesman.com

Vocabulary

gardener

nature

sprout

Word count: 511

Note: The total word count includes words in the running text and headings only.
Numerals and words in chapter titles, captions, labels, diagrams, charts, graphs,
sidebars, and extra features are not included.

Think and Share

1. Tell what happened in the beginning, in the middle, and at the end of this story. Use a chart like the one below to write your answer.

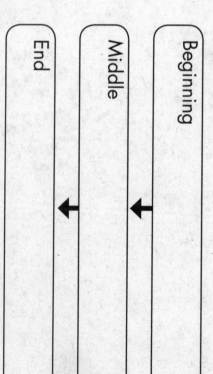

Beginning

Middle

End

2. What phrase on page 8 helps you make a picture in your mind of what Jake's mother looks like when she sees the vine growing?

3. Write at least three words in the book that end in -ed.

4. Jake had a problem to solve. How would you have solved his problem?

The
Mile-a-Minute Vine

by Nancy Day

illustrated by Victor Kennedy

PEARSON

Scott
Foresman

Editorial Offices: Glenview, Illinois • Parsippany, New Jersey • New York, New York
Sales Offices: Needham, Massachusetts • Duluth, Georgia • Glenview, Illinois
Coppell, Texas • Ontario, California • Mesa, Arizona

Kudzu

Mile-a-minute vine is a nickname for the kudzu (KUD-zoo) plant. Kudzu sprouts from a bean. The bean is the seed. It needs some soil, water, and sunlight to grow. Kudzu doesn't grow a mile a minute, but it does grow very fast!

Too much kudzu growing too fast can cause problems. Just like in the story, people have found ways to use this fast-growing and plentiful plant!

Kudzu is growing over this house.

Every effort has been made to secure permission and provide appropriate credit for photographic material. The publisher deeply regrets any omission and pledges to correct errors called to its attention in subsequent editions.

Unless otherwise acknowledged, all photographs are the property of Scott Foresman, a division of Pearson Education.

Photo locators denoted as follows: Top (T), Center (C), Bottom (B), Left (L), Right (R), Background (Bkgd)

Illustrations by Victor Kennedy

ISBN: 0-328-13189-X

2 3 4 5 6 7 8 9 10 V010 14 13 12 11 10 09 08 07 06 05

Next spring, though, the vine turned green and sprang back to life. Jake kept busy. He and his mother did very well in the end!

15

Jake lived with his mother on a farm. It hadn't rained in months. Their peanut crop dried up. They needed money.

"We will have to sell our cow," said Jake's mother.

Jake sighed. "I'll take Bessie into town tomorrow."

3

Jake sold them at a stand by the side of the road. He and the cows kept the vine under control all summer and into the fall.

When the first frost struck, the vine turned brown and dried up. Jake and his mother took a nice vacation.

14

On the way to town, Jake met an old gardener.

"I am going to sell our cow," Jake told the man.

"Why not trade her for these magic beans?" the gardener suggested. "They will grow and grow, rain or not."

Jake made the trade.

But the mile-a-minute vine still covered the field. What could Jake do with it all? He started experimenting. He made mile-a-minute vine jelly, syrup, and tea. He even made baskets out of the vine!

"You traded Bessie for beans?" shouted Jake's mother.

"They are magic beans," Jake replied. "You'll see." He had heard a story about a boy who traded a cow for beans and did very well in the end. Jake planted the beans. Then he sat on the porch to wait.

Cows came from near and far. The old gardener even brought Bessie back. They lifted her up onto Jake's roof! All the cows chewed up the vine as fast as they could. Among them, they ate more than a mile a minute! Houses covered in green went back to normal.

6

Soon, a sprout sprang up. It did not grow up into the sky, like the beanstalk in the story Jake had read. It grew out. The vine grew across the field. It grew right over the tractor. Then it kept on going.

First, Jake tried to pull the root of the vine out of the ground. But the vine just kept growing!

"I have an idea," said Jake. "But I need a cow and Bessie is gone."

"We have cows," said the neighbors.

"Bring them all here," said Jake.

11

The vine grew over everything! It grew up and over some trees. It grew over a stop sign. It even grew over a possum in the field and a sleeping dog!

Then, the mayor rushed up to Jake. "Any plant that grows a mile a minute is against nature," he said. "Do something!"

"I'll do what I can, sir," Jake replied.

8

The vine grew over Jake's porch. Then it grew quickly over the windows and the roof.

"Why is it so dark?" his mother called. She came outside. Her mouth made a round O. "That vine is growing a mile a minute! Go warn the neighbors!"

But the neighbors were already running toward Jake's house.

"Good thing we slammed our windows shut," a woman shouted. "Otherwise, that vine would have wrapped us up inside!"

9

Life Science

Butterflies

by Susan Jones Leeming

Science

Science

Genre	Comprehension Skills and Strategy	Text Features
Expository nonfiction	• Draw Conclusions • Cause and Effect • Text Structure	• Captions • Labels • Glossary

Scott Foresman Reading Street 1.3.5

ISBN 0-328-13192-X

9 780328 131921

90000

PEARSON

Scott
Foresman

scottforesman.com

Vocabulary

cycle

develop

insect

Word count: 416

Note: The total word count includes words in the running text and headings only. Numerals and words in chapter titles, captions, labels, diagrams, charts, graphs, sidebars, and extra features are not included.

Think and Share

1. Reread page 13. Why do you think butterflies lay eggs near flowers?

2. The book talks about the ways butterflies stay safe. What way is talked about first? What way is next? What way is last? Write your answers in a chart like the one below.

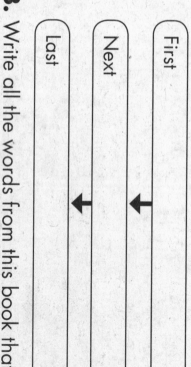

First

Next

Last

3. Write all the words from this book that are contractions. What are the two words that make up each contraction?

4. Which part of the butterfly's life cycle do you like best—the caterpillar, the chrysalis, or the butterfly? Why?

Butterflies

by Susan Jones Leeming

PEARSON
Scott
Foresman

Editorial Offices: Glenview, Illinois • Parsippany, New Jersey • New York, New York
Sales Offices: Needham, Massachusetts • Duluth, Georgia • Glenview, Illinois
Coppell, Texas • Ontario, California • Mesa, Arizona

Glossary

antennae *n.* long, thin feelers on the heads of insects.

camouflage *n.* a shape or color that makes a living thing hard to see.

cycle *n.* something that repeats or moves in the same order over and over again.

develop *v.* to grow.

insect *n.* an animal without bones and with a body in three parts.

nectar *n.* sweet liquid in many flowers.

poisonous *adj.* containing poison.

predators *n.* animals that eat other animals.

protect *v.* to keep safe.

Every effort has been made to secure permission and provide appropriate credit for photographic material. The publisher deeply regrets any omission and pledges to correct errors called to its attention in subsequent editions.

Unless otherwise acknowledged, all photographs are the property of Scott Foresman, a division of Pearson Education.

Photo locators denoted as follows: Top (T), Center (C), Bottom (B), Left (L), Right (R), Background (Bkgd)

Opener: Peter Arnold, Inc.; 1 Aurora & Quanta Productions Inc.; 3 Brand X Pictures; 4 Brand X Pictures; 5 Brand X Pictures; 6 Brand X Pictures; 7 Aurora & Quanta Productions Inc.; 8 Peter Arnold, Inc.; 9 Brand X Pictures; 10 Brand X Pictures; 12 Brand X Pictures; 13 Brand X Pictures; 15 Brand X Pictures;

ISBN: 0-328-13192-X

Here's How to Do It!

1. Find or order caterpillars. If it is the spring or fall, you may be able to find caterpillars on trees or grass near your school. If not, you can order caterpillars on the Internet or from a nature store. Ask an adult for help.

2. Identify the caterpillars. Using a butterfly identification book, match your caterpillars with the ones in the book. Then put them in the home you made for them.

3. Watch for chrysalises to form. Wait for butterflies to emerge. When the butterflies hatch, place fresh flowers and fruit slices into the butterfly box to feed them. On a warm day, release your butterflies into the wild. Watch as they fly away!

Have you ever seen a butterfly flutter by? Have you looked at its colorful wings? Have you watched it land on flowers? Read on to learn about this amazing **insect.**

3

Now Try This

Watching Butterflies Grow

You and your classmates can watch butterflies develop. See them change from caterpillars to chrysalises to beautiful butterflies ready for flight.

You'll need
- a box, large jar, or a terrarium
- a cloth or mesh screen
- branches, dirt, and leaves that your caterpillar likes to eat

14

A butterfly does not begin its life **cycle** as a butterfly. First, there's an egg. When the egg hatches, a caterpillar comes out. The caterpillar eats and eats and eats. Soon it grows large.

Egg

Caterpillar

If their colors aren't enough to **protect** them, butterflies use their wings to fly away. Some butterflies can fly faster than people can run. Once butterflies are safe, they come back to the flowers. There they eat, lay eggs, and begin the life cycle all over again.

When the caterpillar's big enough, it hangs from a branch. Then it changes into a chrysalis. The chrysalis will **develop** into a butterfly.

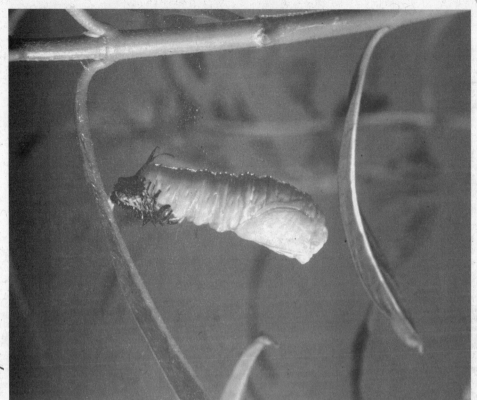

Chrysalis

The bright colors of other butterflies warn enemies that they don't taste good. They may even be **poisonous** or dangerous to eat. These brightly colored butterflies are safe because birds and other insects know they taste bad.

After about two weeks, the waiting is done. The chrysalis has developed into a butterfly. The butterfly pushes out of its old skin. It shivers because its wings are wet. It rests in the sun and waits for its wings to dry.

A butterfly comes out of the chrysalis.

Butterflies are in danger from other insects or animals that want to eat them. Birds and other **predators** try to catch and eat butterflies. Butterflies use their camouflage colors to hide.

Once its wings are dry, the butterfly flies off to find food. Many butterflies eat **nectar,** the sweet juice made by flowers. With its long tongue, a butterfly can suck nectar out of the middle of flowers.

Have you seen the many colors on the wings of a butterfly? The colors make the butterfly beautiful. But beauty is not the only reason the colors are there. The colors help the butterfly. Do you know how? They're **camouflage.** They help the butterfly hide from danger.

Camouflage makes this butterfly hard to see.

Like all insects, the butterfly has two **antennae,** or feelers, on its head. These help the butterfly know what's around it. The butterfly also has feet that help it crawl on flowers. The feet help the butterfly taste too. A butterfly lands on a flower and knows how it tastes!

Feet

Antennae

© Pearson Education, Inc.

A butterfly visits many flowers each day. During the night and on rainy days, the butterfly rests. The butterfly finds a dry branch or leaf to use as a resting place. It may rest there for many hours. This butterfly visits flowers.

Earth Science

Science

Science

Weather or Not

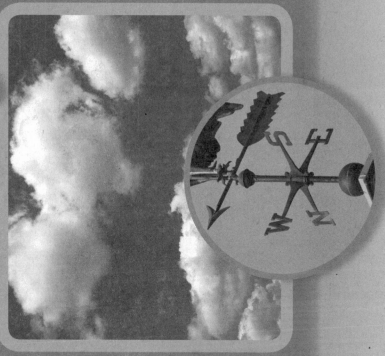

by Nancy Day

Genre	Comprehension Skills and Strategy	Text Features
Expository nonfiction	• Sequence • Author's Purpose • Prior Knowledge	• Captions • Glossary

Scott Foresman Reading Street 1.3.6

PEARSON

Scott
Foresman

scottforesman.com

ISBN 0-328-13195-4

9 780328 131952

90000

Vocabulary

hibernate

predict

season

temperature

Word count: 415

Think and Share

1. What is one thing from folklore that might help people predict rain? Copy the chart onto your paper. Write down one thing you read in the book that happens before it rains.

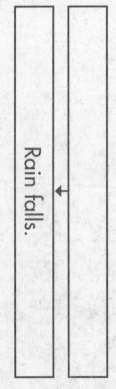

Rain falls.

2. What did you know about making weather predictions before you read this book? How did that help you understand the book?

3. What do birds do when they migrate?

4. Look at the weather sayings in this book. Write a weather saying of your own.

Weather or Not

by Nancy Day

PEARSON

Scott
Foresman

Editorial Offices: Glenview, Illinois • Parsippany, New Jersey • New York, New York
Sales Offices: Needham, Massachusetts • Duluth, Georgia • Glenview, Illinois
Coppell, Texas • Ontario, California • Mesa, Arizona

Glossary

folklore *n.* beliefs, stories, legends, or customs of a people.

forecast *v.* to tell what is going to happen.

hibernate *v.* to spend all winter sleeping or resting.

migrate *v.* to move from one place to another.

predict *v.* to tell about something before it happens.

season *n.* one of the four parts of the year: winter, spring, summer, or autumn.

temperature *n.* how hot or cold something is.

16

Every effort has been made to secure permission and provide appropriate credit for photographic material. The publisher deeply regrets any omission and pledges to correct errors called to its attention in subsequent editions.

Unless otherwise acknowledged, all photographs are the property of Scott Foresman, a division of Pearson Education.

Photo locators denoted as follows: Top (T), Center (C), Bottom (B), Left (L), Right (R), Background (Bkgd)

Opener: (C) Getty Images, (B) Creatas; 1 (B) Creatas, (C) Getty Images; 3 (C) The Image Works, Inc., (BR) Brand X Pictures; 4 (TR) ©Comstock Inc., (C) ©Royalty-Free/Corbis; 5 (C) Brand X Pictures, (BR) Creatas; 6 (BR) Thinkstock, (C) Getty Images; 7 (TR) Thinkstock, (C) ©Royalty-Free/Corbis; 8 (TL) Creatas, (C) Getty Images; 9 (TR) Brand X Pictures, (C) Getty Images; 10 (C) Kennan Ward/Corbis, (BR) Brand X Pictures; 11 (TR) Gene J. Puskar/APWide World Photos, (C) Gene J. Puskar/APWide World Photos; 12 (TL) Brand X Pictures, (C) Digital Vision; 13 (TR) ©Royalty-Free/Corbis, (C) Getty Images; 14 Creatas; 15 Getty Images

ISBN: 0-328-13195-4

2 3 4 5 6 7 8 9 10 V010 14 13 12 11 10 09 08 07 06 05

Here's How to Do It!

1. If you can hear crickets in the evening, ask an adult to take you outside.
2. Use a thermometer to find out the temperature and write it down.
3. Count how many chirps you hear in 15 seconds.
4. Add 40 to the number of chirps. The total should be close to what the thermometer says.

A stopwatch can help keep track of time.

How did people **predict** the weather in the past? They judged the coming weather by using clues around them. They made up sayings and tales from what they noticed. Over time, some of these sayings and tales about weather became **folklore.**

In the past, people used almanacs to find out about the weather. Today, we get weather information on the news report.

Now Try This

Crickets as Weather Forecasters

Weather folklore says you can tell the temperature outside by counting cricket chirps. This works because crickets chirp faster in warm weather.

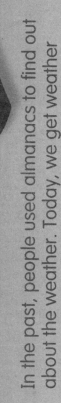

A cricket

People have looked at the sky, sun, and clouds to **forecast** the weather. Sailors have always needed to know how the weather might change. This old sailor's rhyme is often true:

Some people believe that animals may act differently right before a storm. Here is some folklore about animals and weather:

"If a dog whines for no reason, look for a storm."

"Birds flying low, expect rain and a blow."

"Frogs croak before a rain, but in the sun are quiet again."

4

4   13

"Red sky by morning, sailor take warning. Red sky at night, sailor's delight." Usually, a red sky in the morning means clouds are on the way. A red sky at night means the clouds have already passed by.

Some people watch animals to guess the **temperature.** When each **season** changes, some people look at what animals do. Watching birds **migrate** south for the winter sometimes tells people it will be cold soon. What can people tell when the birds come back?

"The higher the clouds, the fairer the weather."

Water and snow do not usually fall from the kinds of clouds that are high in the sky. So looking at the sky can help make a weather prediction.

Groundhog Day is a fun tradition. But it is not a good weather predictor. It has been wrong almost twice as often as it has been right!

Groundhog Day celebration in Pennsylvania

However, not all weather sayings are about looking at the sky.

"Doors and drawers stick before the rain falls."

Extra water in the air can make wood swell to a larger size. Then wooden doors and drawers can get stuck in place.

A well-known animal forecaster is the groundhog. Groundhogs **hibernate** in winter. On February 2, a groundhog is said to wake up and pop out from underground. If he sees his shadow, winter will last six more weeks.

People's bodies can sometimes predict rain. Curly hair may curl more. Some people say their joints hurt more before it rains.

Some people use plants to get clues about rain too. Flowers have the strongest smell right before it rains.

Tree leaves grow with their shiny side facing the sun. The wind that comes before a storm blows them so that you can see their lighter green backs.

Cascarones Are for Fun

by Sammie Witt

illustrated by Sue Frankenberry

Suggested levels for Guided Reading, DRA,™
Lexile,® and Reading Recovery™ are provided
in the Pearson Scott Foresman Leveling Guide.

Genre	Comprehension Skill and Strategy	Text Features
Narrative nonfiction	• Draw Conclusions • Sequence • Monitor and Fix-Up	• Glossary • Headings

Scott Foresman Reading Street 1.4.1

PEARSON

Scott
Foresman

scottforesman.com

ISBN 0-328-13198-9

9 780328 131983

90000

Vocabulary

celebrate
cherish
China
confetti
decorate
empress
Italy
Mexico
perfume

Word count: 534

Note: The total word count includes words in the running text and headings only. Numerals and words in chapter titles, captions, labels, diagrams, charts, graphs, sidebars, and extra features are not included.

Think and Share

1. After learning about cascarones, would you want to make one? Use details from the book to explain why or why not.

2. What would you tell classmates to do so they could better understand what they are reading?

3. Choose one of these words from the story: celebrate, grateful, cherish. Write it in the center of a web like the one below. What other words does this word make you think of? Add them to the web.

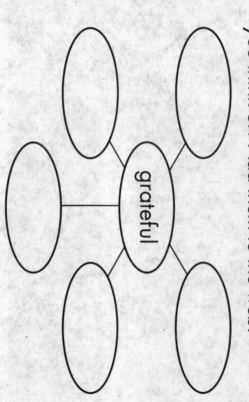

grateful

4. Retell what you learned about cascarones by answering the questions that are on pages 6, 9, and 12.

Cascarones Are for Fun

by Sammie Witt
illustrated by Sue Frankenberry

PEARSON
Scott Foresman

Editorial Offices: Glenview, Illinois • Parsippany, New Jersey • New York, New York
Sales Offices: Needham, Massachusetts • Duluth, Georgia • Glenview, Illinois
Coppell, Texas • Ontario, California • Mesa, Arizona

Glossary

celebrate *v.* to have a party for a special event or day

cherish *v.* to like or care about something or someone very deeply

China *n.* a large Asian country that is far from the United States

confetti *n.* tiny bits of brightly colored paper

decorate *v.* to fix something up to make it look special by painting, coloring, or trimming it with bits of things

empress *n.* a title for a woman who is the highest ruler of a country

Italy *n.* a country across the Atlantic Ocean from the United States

Mexico *n.* a country that shares the border with the southern part of the United States

perfume *n.* a liquid, like water, that smells sweet

Every effort has been made to secure permission and provide appropriate credit for photographic material. The publisher deeply regrets any omission and pledges to correct errors called to its attention in subsequent editions.

Unless otherwise acknowledged, all photographs are the property of Scott Foresman, a division of Pearson Education.

ISBN: 0-328-13198-9

Think about the ways you might cook your eggs. Then talk with classmates and family about the different ways to cook eggs.

Now you are ready to make a cookbook about eggs.

15

Cascarones are made from eggshells. But what about the leftover egg inside? Eggs are a very good food. Do you know any ways to cook eggs?

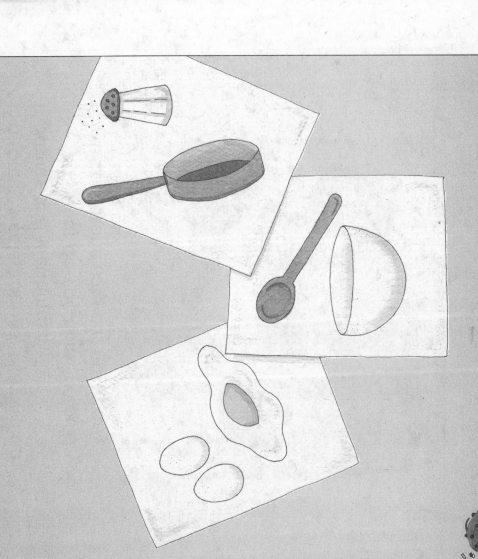

What Are Cascarones?

See the eggshells in the picture? These special eggshells are called cascarones. Cascarones is a Spanish word that means "shells." You say the word like this: kas-ka-ron-nez.

In this book you will find out about cascarones and why they are so much fun.

The cascarones look pretty, don't they? Would you be surprised to learn that people are supposed to break them? And they not only break them, but they break them over one another's heads!

But don't worry. No real egg will get on people's heads. Cascarones are made with just the eggshells.

The Mexican people also use cascarones on the Fifth of May. That day is an important day for Mexico. It celebrates the day Mexico became a country. It is like our Fourth of July celebration.

Cascarones can also be a part of a family's celebrations, like birthday parties and weddings.

So, what do you think? Would you like cascarones at your next party?

4

13

In Mexico and parts of the United States, people use cascarones to **celebrate** special days.

On those days, children love to surprise friends and family by cracking the cascarones over their heads. No one gets mad when the eggs are broken over them. They are grateful because the eggshells and the stuff inside bring good luck.

When Are Cascarones Used Today?

Cascarones are still used in Mexico. They have also become popular in certain parts of the United States.

In Mexico, cascarones are used in different celebrations. A really big one is a festival called Carnival. That festival happens in the spring.

How Are Cascarones Made?

Here is a family making cascarones. First, they make small holes in both ends of an egg. Then, they blow the raw egg from inside the shell out into a bowl.

Afterward, they clean the eggshells with water and let them safely dry. When the empty eggshells are ready, people **decorate** the shells by painting them.

Other countries soon came to **cherish** the filled eggs as well.

The idea of these special eggs was brought to **Mexico** by the **Empress** Carlotta. She and her husband ruled Mexico more than 150 years ago.

Some say that Empress Carlotta was the first person who had the eggshells filled with confetti instead of perfume and powder.

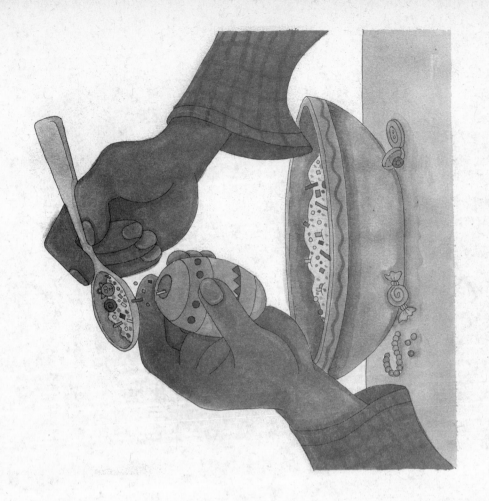

After the paint is dry, the cascarones are filled with **confetti** and small toys. Confetti is tiny pieces of colored paper. The confetti flies out when the eggshells are cracked open.

These eggs became popular in Italy. Young men would toss the eggs to young women. Sometimes the eggs broke, and the woman would get covered in the perfume or powder.

The holes in each filled eggshell are closed with a small piece of tape.

Now the cascarones are ready for the celebration—and so are the people who made them!

Who Brought the First Cascarones?

Long ago, there was a famous explorer named Marco Polo. He was from **Italy**.

Marco Polo went all over the world and brought many things back from his travels.

One of the things he brought back were special eggs from **China**. These eggs were like cascarones. But they were not filled with confetti. They were filled with **perfume** or powder.

Suggested levels for Guided Reading, DRA,™
Lexile® and Reading Recovery™ are provided
in the Pearson Scott Foresman Leveling Guide.

Susan's Missing Painting

by Lana Rios
Illustrated by Jeff Hopkins

Genre	Comprehension Skills and Strategy	
Realistic fiction	• Theme • Character, Setting, Plot • Graphic Organizers	

Scott Foresman Reading Street 1.4.2

PEARSON
Scott
Foresman

scottforesman.com

Vocabulary

create
doodle
imagination

Word count: 757

Note: The total word count includes words in the running text and headings only.
Numerals and words in chapter titles, captions, labels, diagrams, charts, graphs,
sidebars, and extra features are not included.

Think and Share

1. What is the big idea of this story?

2. Think about what happened in the story.
   Copy the chart on your paper.
   Fill in what happened.

   Title: Susan's Missing Painting

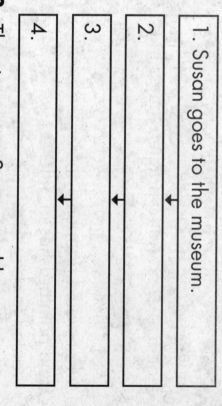

1. Susan goes to the museum.

2.

3.

4.

3. The story says Susan used her
   imagination to decide what to paint.
   What do you think this means?

4. How do you think Susan felt when she
   saw her painting at the art show? How
   would you have felt if you were Susan?

Susan's Missing Painting

By Lana Rios
Illustrated by Jeff Hopkins

PEARSON

Scott
Foresman

Editorial Offices: Glenview, Illinois • Parsippany, New Jersey • New York, New York
Sales Offices: Needham, Massachusetts • Duluth, Georgia • Glenview, Illinois
Coppell, Texas • Ontario, California • Mesa, Arizona

Georges Seurat

Georges Seurat was born in Paris, France, in 1859. He began drawing when he was a teenager. He went to art school when he was nineteen years old.

Seurat painted many things that people could see in daily life. He painted people at the beach. He painted vases and lighthouses. He also painted things that were special events, like circuses.

At that time, artists were trying to see what would happen if they used paint and paintbrushes in different ways. Seurat wanted to show light in many ways in a picture. He used tiny brush strokes of pure color. These dots are too small to see when you look at the whole picture. You can only see them when you look closely at part of the picture. These dots are what give the pictures their special feeling.

Every effort has been made to secure permission and provide appropriate credit for photographic material. The publisher deeply regrets any omission and pledges to correct errors called to its attention in subsequent editions.

Unless otherwise acknowledged, all photographs are the property of Scott Foresman, a division of Pearson Education.

16 ©Frank Scherschel/Time Life Pictures/Getty Images

ISBN: 0-328-13201-2

© Pearson Education, Inc.

That night Susan went to a party at the art show. Her whole family came, even her grandparents.

"I always knew you would be a great artist," said her grandma.

A lot of people looked at Susan's painting.

A lady came up to Susan. "Can I buy your picture?" she asked.

"I'm sorry," said Susan. "I am giving it to my grandma."

When Susan was one year old, her grandma gave her a present. It was a pack of crayons. Susan loved her crayons. She loved them so much that she ate the red one, the blue one, and part of the yellow one.

Susan got her next pack of crayons when she was three years old. This time she knew what to do with all the colors. This time she began to draw.

Susan walked to school the next day. She felt sad about her missing painting. She stopped in front of the place that always had the art shows.

Susan looked in the window. Then she looked again. Susan smiled. She could not believe it! There was her painting. It was next to a sign that said, "Young Artists—Opening Tonight."

"I wanted to surprise you," said her mother.

When Susan was seven, she was making art all the time. She painted before breakfast. She even drew at the dinner table.

Sometimes Susan drew things that she saw. Sometimes she used her imagination and made up things. Her grandma said, "You will be a great artist one day."

Susan looked everywhere for her painting.

She looked in her closet. She looked under her bed. She even looked in with the dirty clothes.

"Mom!" cried Susan. "Where is my painting? I looked all over and I can't find it anywhere."

"Oh," said her mom. "Don't worry about the picture. I'm sure it will turn up."

Susan passed a special place every day on her way to school. This place had art shows. Susan always stopped to stare at the paintings.

Some paintings made her feel happy. Some paintings made her feel sad. And some made her want to think about things.

"Hurry up!" her mother would say. Susan was late for school a lot.

The next week Susan did not have school. She went to visit her grandma and grandpa.

Before she went home, her grandpa said, "Soon it will be Grandma's birthday. You know that she loves your pictures. Maybe you can make her a painting."

Susan thought that was a great idea. She decided to give Grandma her dot painting. But when she got home, she could not find her picture.

One day Susan's teacher, Ms. Ito, said, "I have a surprise. We are going to the art museum."

At the museum, some of the children poked each other. Some tried to run around. Those children got in trouble and had to sit down.

"Please, everybody," said Ms. Ito. "Find a picture you really like. Then look at it for a while."

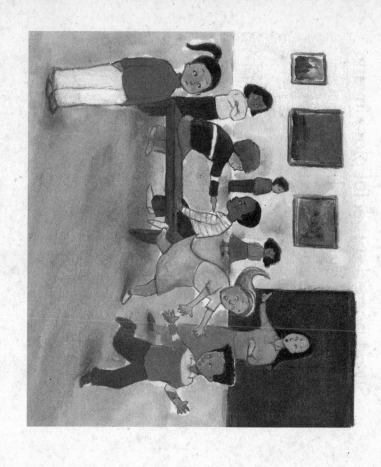

6

Nobody bothered Susan while she painted. She painted for a very long time. At last she was done.

"Come and see my picture," she called to her parents.

"It is wonderful," said her mother.

"It is amazing," said her father.

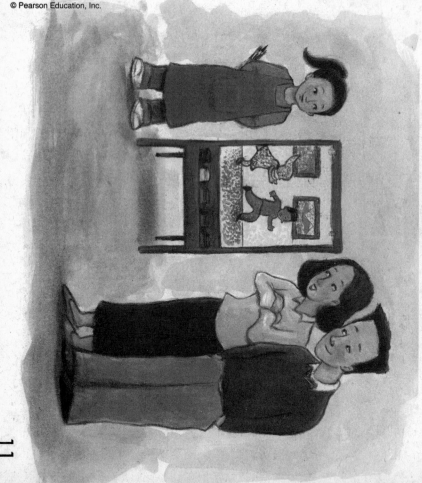

Susan looked at all the paintings in the room. Then she found the one she liked the best. It was a painting of a circus.

Susan thought about the picture of the circus. Then she thought about how the children were running around in the museum. She decided it would be fun to make a picture of that.

She drew an outline of what she wanted to paint. She dipped a small brush into some paint. She made a dot on the paper.

Susan used many colors and made many dots.

At first it looked like most paintings. Then Susan stood close to it. She stared at the picture.

"It is made out of tiny dots!" she said.

"That painting is by a man called Georges Seurat" said Ms. Ito. "He used tiny spots of color to make his picture."

"It is so beautiful! And it looks fun," said Susan. "I want to create a painting like that."

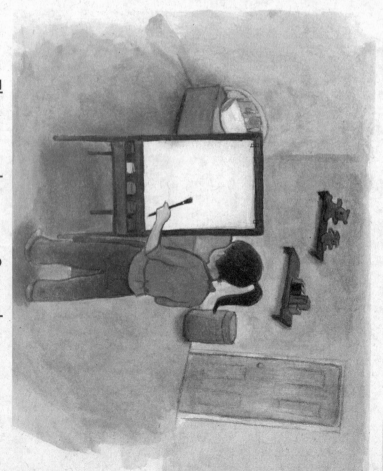

The next day was Saturday.

"I will be very busy today," Susan told her parents. "I am going to paint with dots."

"Oh my," said Susan's mother. She went into the other room and left Susan alone to work.

Susan took out her pencils and paints. She took out her brushes. She set up her easel. She looked at the easel for a long time.

Earth Science

Science

Science

Finding a Dinosaur Named Sue

by Beth Lewis

Suggested levels for Guided Reading, DRA™,
Lexile®, and Reading Recovery™ are provided
in the Pearson Scott Foresman Leveling Guide.

Genre	Comprehension Skills and Strategy	Text Features
Expository nonfiction	• Author's Purpose • Cause and Effect • Monitor and Fix Up	• Captions • Glossary

Scott Foresman Reading Street 1.4.3

ISBN 0-328-13204-7

9 780328 132041

90000

PEARSON

Scott
Foresman

scottforesman.com

Vocabulary

auction

evidence

excavate

fossils

skilled

skull

soil

wishbone

Word count: 615

Note: The total word count includes words in the running text and headings only. Numerals and words in chapter titles, captions, labels, diagrams, charts, graphs, sidebars, and extra features are not included.

Think and Share

1. Why do you think the author wrote this book?

2. What questions about dinosaurs would you like to look up after reading this book? Where will you look?

3. On a separate sheet of paper make a T-chart. Write all the words from the book that end with –ing in the left column. Next to each word in the right column, write the base word.

-ing word	Base word

4. Name a fact that you learned just from reading one of the picture captions.

Finding a Dinosaur Named Sue

by Beth Lewis

Editorial Offices: Glenview, Illinois • Parsippany, New Jersey • New York, New York
Sales Offices: Needham, Massachusetts • Duluth, Georgia • Glenview, Illinois
Coppell, Texas • Ontario, California • Mesa, Arizona

Glossary

auction *n.* a public sale in which a thing is sold to the one who offers the most money for it

evidence *n.* something that gives proof

excavate *v.* uncover by digging

fossils *n.* the rock-like remains of plants or animals that lived long ago

skilled *adj.* being able to do something well

skull *n.* the skeletal frame of the head

soil *n.* the loose top layer of the Earth's surface

wishbone *n.* the forked bone in front of the breastbone in most birds

Every effort has been made to secure permission and provide appropriate credit for photographic material. The publisher deeply regrets any omission and pledges to correct errors called to its attention in subsequent editions.

Unless otherwise acknowledged, all photographs are the property of Scott Foresman, a division of Pearson Education.

Photo locators denoted as follows: Top (T), Center (C), Bottom (B), Left (L), Right (R), Background (Bkgd)

Cover ©Jim Zuckerman/Corbis; 1 ©Layne Kennedy/Corbis; 3 (TL) ©Layne Kennedy/Corbis, 3 (TR) ©JOHN ZICH/AFP/Getty Images; 6 ©The Field Museum.GN88537_12c; 7 ©The Field Museum.GN89086_19c; 8 (Bkgd) © Layne Kennedy/Corbis, 8 (BL) © Layne Kennedy/Corbis; 9 ©The Field Museum.GEO86195_3c; 10-11 ©The Field Museum. GN89714_2RDC, 10 (CL) ©The Field Museum.GN89714_2RDC, 11 (BR) ©The Field Museum.GN89714_2RDC; 12 (TL) ©Joseph Sohm; ChromoSohm Inc./Corbis, 12 (TR) ©The Field Museum.GN98808_43c; 13 (TR) ©Reuters/Corbis, 13 (CL) ©Reuters/Corbis

ISBN: 0-328-13204-7

2 3 4 5 6 7 8 9 10 V010 14 13 12 11 10 09 08 07 06 05

- On the other side of the card, write the fact that answers the question. Next to it, draw a picture of your answer.

- Exchange fact cards with a partner. Try to answer each question. Look on the other side of the card to see if your answer was right.

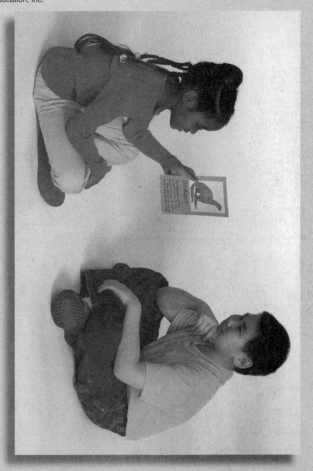

Sue Hendrickson discovered the bones of a tyrannosaurus rex.

In the summer of 1990, Sue Hendrickson made a big discovery on a ranch in South Dakota near the Cheyenne River.

One day, Sue saw some small pieces of bone on the ground. She climbed a cliff to see where the **fossils,** the remains of ancient animals, had come from. There, Sue found huge dinosaur bones!

Sue thought the bones were from a tyrannosaurus rex. She was right. The rest of the team saw what she found. They named it "Sue," because Sue Hendrickson found the dinosaur bones.

Now Try This

Fact Cards for Sue

- Use the information that you learned about Sue to make five fact cards.
- On one side of a card, write a question about Sue.

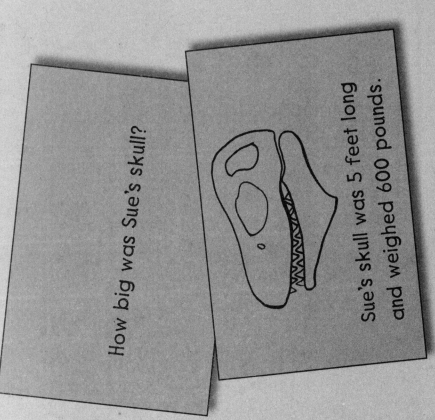

How big was Sue's skull?

Sue's skull was 5 feet long and weighed 600 pounds.

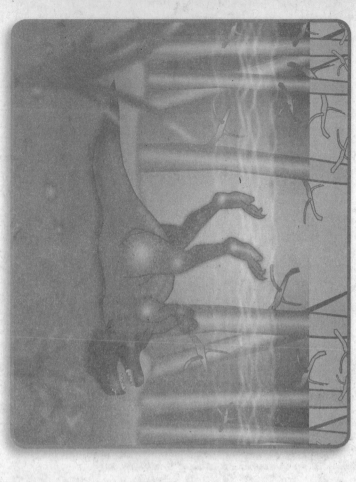

Sue got buried by sand and soil after she died.

The dinosaur named Sue died about 65 million years ago. As time went by, her bones were covered with sand and **soil.** The sand and soil became rock, and Sue's bones became fossils. More time passed. The rock got worn away. Then Sue's bones were found.

One question that people often ask is, "Was Sue a female?" The answer is that no one knows whether Sue was a female or male. Maybe that question and others will be answered in the future, as scientists continue to study the dinosaur named Sue.

It took the team only 17 days to **excavate** Sue's bones. That was because all the bones were found in one place. They used many tools, such as shovels, picks, and rock hammers. When they got closer to the bones, they used smaller tools.

The team found more than 200 bones. That made Sue the most complete T. rex ever to be discovered!

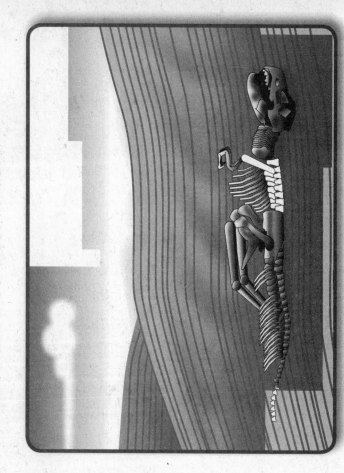

Over millions of years, Sue's bones turned into fossils.

Sue is one of the most popular displays at the Field Museum.

At last, on May 17, 2000, Sue went on display at the Field Museum. Sue is a very special and important exhibit. It is the largest and best preserved T. rex that has ever been found. It is also the most complete tyrannosaurus rex, because more than 200 bones were found.

A museum in Chicago bought Sue.

After Sue was excavated, many people disagreed about who owned her. It took about five years for the courts to make a decision. They decided that Sue's owner was the rancher who owned the land where Sue was found.

The rancher decided to sell Sue at an **auction.** The auction took place in 1997. The Field Museum in Chicago paid 8 million dollars for Sue at the auction.

Scientists found that Sue had a **wishbone.** This may mean that dinosaurs are related to birds, but it does not prove it. There has to be more **evidence** before we can know for sure.

Can you see Sue's wishbone in this picture?

© Pearson Education, Inc.

There was a lot of work to do before people could see Sue at the museum. A team of people worked to prepare Sue's bones and put her together. These people were **skilled** at their jobs. Their goal was to clean each fossil bone and glue the broken bones together. It was like putting together a very big puzzle!

A tool called an "air scribe" is used to remove rock from the bones.

Two bumps show that Sue broke this rib twice.

Scientists took x-rays and learned that Sue had broken ribs. The x-rays showed that Sue's ribs had two bumps on them. Scientists know that a broken bone often heals by growing new bone. The new bone causes a bump to form.

It took seven people more than 3,500 hours to clean and put together Sue's **skull**. When they were done, it measured five feet long. It weighed more than 600 pounds!

The team found that Sue's mouth had 58 large, sharp teeth when she was living. The teeth were between seven inches and one foot long!

The team worked more on Sue's skull than on any other part.

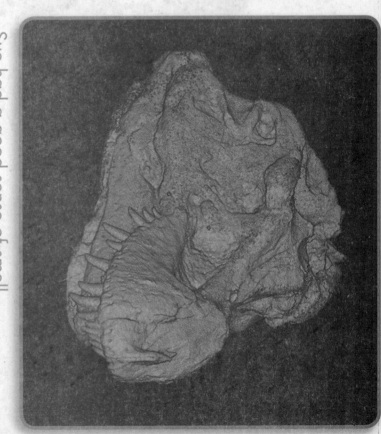

Sue had a good sense of smell.

Scientists took a special x-ray of Sue's skull, called a CT image. They found that a large part of Sue's brain was used for smelling. That told the scientists that a tyrannosaurus rex had a very good sense of smell.

Scientists learned that both of Sue's eyes faced forward. That told them that a tyrannosaurus rex could see how far away something to eat was.

Suggested levels for Guided Reading, DRA™,
Lexile®, and Reading Recovery™ are provided
in the Pearson Scott Foresman Leveling Guide.

The Moon Lady and Her Festival

by Libby McCord

illustrated by CD Hullinger

Genre	Comprehension Skills and Strategy
Legend	• Realism and Fantasy • Theme • Monitor and Fix-Up

Scott Foresman Reading Street 1.4.4

PEARSON

Scott
Foresman

scottforesman.com

Vocabulary

delightful
festive
symbol

Word count: 635

Note: The total word count includes words in the running text and headings only. Numerals and words in chapter titles, captions, labels, diagrams, charts, graphs, sidebars, and extra features are not included.

Think and Share

1. What parts of this story are real and what parts are made up?

2. What can you do if you don't understand what part the rabbit plays on page 8?

3. Make a web with Moon Festival in the center. Around it write words that go with Moon Festival.

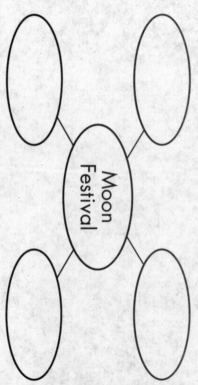

4. What did you like best about Chang-O's story? What would you like to do to celebrate the Moon Festival?

The Moon Lady and Her Festival

by Libby McCord

illustrated by CD Hullinger

PEARSON
Scott
Foresman

Editorial Offices: Glenview, Illinois • Parsippany, New Jersey • New York, New York
Sales Offices: Needham, Massachusetts • Duluth, Georgia • Glenview, Illinois
Coppell, Texas • Ontario, California • Mesa, Arizona

The Moon Festival

The Moon Festival is very important in China. You have read one Moon Festival story. There are many other stories as well. One story is about moon cakes.

A long time ago the Chinese were under the rule of the Mongols. The Mongols were cruel to the Chinese. The Chinese decided to fight against them. During one Moon Festival, the Chinese bakers hid messages in the moon cakes. The messages told people when to fight the Mongols.

The start of the fighting suprised the Mongols. The Chinese won, so they were no longer ruled by the Mongols. This story is one reason that moon cakes are important to Chinese culture.

16

ISBN: 0-328-13207-1

Copyright © Pearson Education, Inc.

All Rights Reserved. Printed in the United States of America. This publication is protected by Copyright, and permission should be obtained from the publisher prior to any prohibited reproduction, storage in a retrieval system, or transmission in any form by any means, electronic, mechanical, photocopying, recording, or likewise. For information regarding permission(s), write to: Permissions Department, Scott Foresman, 1900 East Lake Avenue, Glenview, Illinois 60025.

2 3 4 5 6 7 8 9 10 V010 14 13 12 11 10 09 08 07 06 05

People eat moon cakes with a boiled egg in the middle. Some cakes have a picture of the moon rabbit on top.

Families get together and have fun. They tell stories about the moon. Then they eat lots of moon cakes!

15

Long ago, in China, there was a man named Yi. Yi was a great archer. He had a beautiful wife named Chang-O. Yi and Chang-O loved each other very much.

One day, ten suns shone and the earth became very dry. So the ruler asked Yi to shoot down nine of the suns.

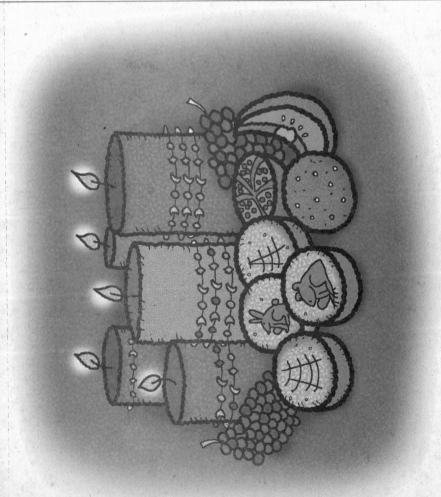

At the Moon Festival, people put out bowls of water to reflect the moon. They light candles and read moon poems. People also have foods that are symbols of the moon. They have round fruit, like grapes, peaches, and melons.

Yi knocked all but one sun out of the sky. That sun shines on Earth today. As thanks, Yi got a magic pill. It would let him live forever! But, first, he had to pray for a year to get ready for the magic. Yi hid the pill in his house.

People celebrate the Moon Festival in many ways. They make pictures of the moon goddess. They put on puppet shows about Chang-O and Yi. Children like Chang-O because they think she knows about their secret wishes.

When Chang-O was home alone, she smelled a delightful smell. She followed her nose. Then she saw a beam of light coming through a crack.

It was the magic pill. Chang-O ate it to see what would happen.

Chinese people look up at the full moon and still think of this story. Every year, they tell it to their children during the Moon Festival.

The Moon Festival also celebrates the end of harvest. People give thanks for what they have.

Just then, Yi came home. He saw Chang-O floating out the window.

"No!" Yi cried. "Do not go away!"

"I was wrong, but I cannot stop!" she called back.

After their day together the two had to part.

"Good-bye!" Chang-O waved.

"Good-bye!" called Yi. He flew back to the sun.

They longed for each other—until the next full moon.

Chang-O flew up into the night sky. Yi chased her as far as he could. But the winds blew him back to Earth.

Chang-O flew straight up to the moon! She shivered. The moon was a cold, silent place, full of dusty rocks.

Yi was allowed to visit Chang-O on the night of the full moon every month. Yi and Chang-O built the Palace of Great Cold. The outside walls were silver. Inside, the rooms were the colors of the rainbow.

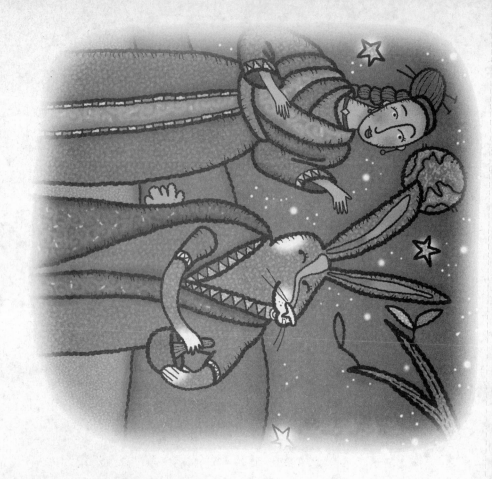

Chang-O met a rabbit under a tree.
"Hello," said Chang-O. "Is it always
cold here?"
"Always," the rabbit said.
"Do you know how to make me a
special drink so I can go back to Earth?"
asked Chang-O.

The rabbit tried, but he could not
make the right drink. So Chang-O could
not fly. She had to stay there forever.
She became goddess of the moon.
Yi became the god of the sun and
lived in the Palace of the Sun.

Double Trouble

by June Edelstein

illustrated by Tom McKee

Genre	Comprehension Skills and Strategy
Realistic fiction	• Character, Setting, Plot • Realism and Fantasy • Story Structure

Scott Foresman Reading Street 1.4.5

ISBN 0-328-13210-1

9 780328 132102

90000

PEARSON

Scott
Foresman

scottforesman.com

Think and Share

1. Complete a story map like the one below.

Double Trouble
Characters:
Setting:
Plot:

2. What happens at the beginning, middle, and end of this story?

3. Write five compound words from the story. Draw a line between the two smaller words in each compound.

4. If you are a twin, what do you like and dislike about being a twin? If you are not a twin, what do you think you would like and dislike about being a twin?

Vocabulary

jealous

relatives

sibling

Word count: 890

Note: The total word count includes words in the running text and headings only. Numerals and words in chapter titles, captions, labels, diagrams, charts, graphs, sidebars, and extra features are not included.

Double Trouble

by June Edelstein
illustrated by Tom McKee

PEARSON

Scott
Foresman

Editorial Offices: Glenview, Illinois • Parsippany, New Jersey • New York, New York
Sales Offices: Needham, Masachusetts • Duluth, Georgia • Glenview, Illinois
Coppell, Texas • Ontario, California • Mesa, Arizona

Twins

There are two kinds of twins. One kind looks alike. They are called identical twins. This kind is always two boys or two girls. The other kind of twins can be two boys, two girls, or a boy and a girl. They may or may not look alike. Many people think that twins have a special relationship.

Stories about twins have been around for a long time. The Navajo Indians have a myth, or story, about twins who free the Earth from monsters. In West Africa, a myth tells about twins, Mawa and Liza, who created the world.

Apollo and Artemis are famous twins from Greek myths. Apollo is the god of light, archery, healing, and music. Artemis is the goddess of the moon, hunting, and giving birth.

16

ISBN: 0-328-13210-1

Copyright © Pearson Education, Inc.

All Rights Reserved. Printed in the United States of America. This publication is protected by Copyright, and permission should be obtained from the publisher prior to any prohibited reproduction, storage in a retrieval system, or transmission in any form by any means, electronic, mechanical, photocopying, recording, or likewise. For information regarding permission(s), write to: Permissions Department, Scott Foresman, 1900 East Lake Avenue, Glenview, Illinois 60025.

2 3 4 5 6 7 8 9 10 V010 14 13 12 11 10 09 08 07 06 05

That evening, Sam and Peter's mother came home from shopping. She saw that the vase was gone and looked at the twins.

"We broke your vase," said Peter. "We were both at fault. We are going to try to be more careful."

"We earned money to fix the vase," said Sam. "We know it is one of your treasures."

"Oh, thank you" said their mother, giving them both a hug. "That vase is a treasure, but you two are my biggest treasures of all."

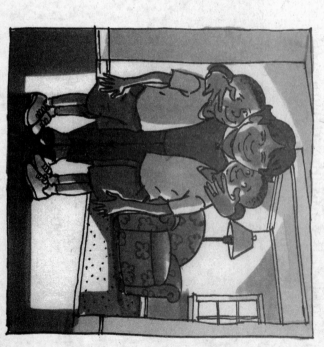

15

Peter and Sam were siblings. They weren't just siblings. They were twins. In fact they were not just twins, they were twins who got into a lot of trouble. "Double Trouble" their mother called them.

Now, it's not that they were bad. It's just that trouble followed them around.

"It is Tim's fault," said Tina every time.

"It is Tina's fault," said Tim every time.

"You are both at fault," said Peter finally.

"Yes," said Sam. "And could you please be a little more careful?"

Then Sam looked at Peter. Peter looked at Sam. They started laughing.

"Maybe we can learn from Tina and Tim," said Sam.

"I think so," said Peter.

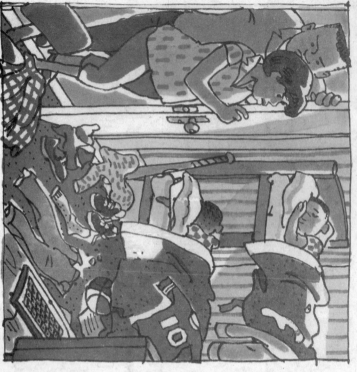

"Time to get up," called their mother.

"Breakfast is ready," said their father.

"Mmmphhh," mumbled Peter, not moving.

"Snurrrgle," mumbled Sam, not moving either.

"Time to get up RIGHT NOW!" said their mother firmly. "I don't want you to be late for school."

"If you don't get up right now," said their father, "I am going to eat all of the blueberry pancakes."

"Oh no," said Sam. "Double trouble."

"It was Tim's idea," said Tina.

"It was Tina's idea," said Tim.

The whole afternoon went like that.

Tim and Tina tried to see how many plates they could balance on their heads. Luckily, Peter caught the plates.

Then Tina and Tim tried to see how long it would take to fill the kitchen sink. Luckily, Sam found the mop.

The twins loved blueberry pancakes. They got up right away. Maybe it was a little too fast.

Sam got mixed up in his blankets and pillows. The blankets and pillows fell out of the bed. Sam fell off of the ladder.

Peter was already out of bed. The blankets and pillows fell on Peter. THUNK! Then Sam fell on Peter. THUMP!

Peter fell against the table. The lamp on the table fell to the floor. CRASH!

"We can take care of twins," said Sam and Peter.

"You're hired," the neighbor said and went upstairs.

Tim and Tina were kicking a ball in the living room. The ball sailed through the air. It was heading toward the television. Sam caught the ball just in time.

"Kicking a ball in the house is a bad idea," said Peter to Tim and Tina.

Sam and Peter's mother looked at the mess. She shook her head. She was not happy.

"Why does this always happen?" she asked. She wasn't really expecting an answer. She got one anyway.

"Sam never thinks about what he is doing," said Peter.

"Peter never thinks about what he is doing," said Sam.

"Do too," said Peter. "It's your fault!"

"Do not," said Sam. "It's your fault!"

A new family had just moved in next door. Maybe they needed some help.

"Do you have any work we can do?" asked Sam. "We can rake leaves."

"Hmm," said the neighbor. "I do need some help but not with the leaves. I need someone to play with Tim and Tina while I go upstairs and unpack some boxes."

"Tim and Tina?" asked Peter.

"They are my five-year-old twins," said the neighbor. "Sometimes they get into trouble."

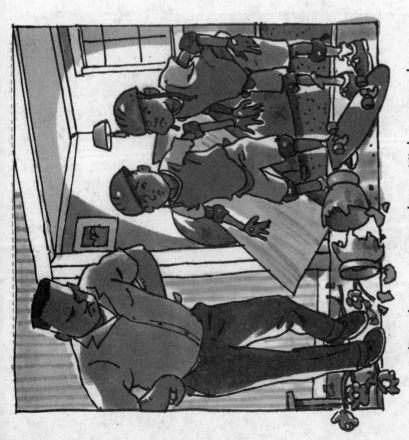

"What have you done!" he cried.

"That is your mother's favorite vase."

"It was Sam's idea," said Peter.

"It was Peter's idea," said Sam.

"I don't care whose idea it was," said their father. "Just make this better."

The twins were sorry they broke their mother's vase. It would make her sad. They decided they should earn some money and get the vase fixed. That would be a good surprise.

"Remember when our relatives were here for Thanksgiving?" said Peter. "You knocked the turkey right off the plate."

"You should have caught the ball," said Sam. "And what about the time you kicked over that can of paint?"

"You were chasing me," said Peter.

"You were jealous because I can run faster. It was your fault!"

"No," said Sam. "It was your fault! You do not run faster than I do."

"Hey! That's enough," said their father.

That's what life with the twins was like. There were a lot of messes, and broken things, and arguments about whose fault it was.

Things went on this way until one rainy day when their mother was out shopping. Their father was in the basement fixing Peter's table. The twins didn't know what to do. Then they had an idea about using their skateboards and the chair. It was not a good idea.

8

The twins built a ramp on the chair. They went down the ramp on their skateboards. They went way too fast. They fell off of the skateboards! But one skateboard kept going. It kept going until it hit their mother's vase. The vase went CRASH! The twins' father could hear the crash all the way in the basement. He came running upstairs.

9

Special Buildings

by Lana Cruce

Social Studies

Genre	Comprehension Skills and Strategy	Text Features
Expository nonfiction	• Cause and Effect • Draw Conclusions • Preview the Text	• Captions • Glossary

Scott Foresman Reading Street 1.4.6

PEARSON
Scott Foresman

scottforesman.com

ISBN 0-328-13213-6

9 780328 132133

90000

Vocabulary

discover

dwell

gargoyle

government

griffin

resident

welcome

Word count: 555

Note: The total word count includes words in the running text and headings only. Numerals and words in chapter titles, captions, labels, diagrams, charts, graphs, sidebars, and extra features are not included.

Think and Share

1. Look at pages 6 and 7. What was the effect of putting a gargoyle on a building? Use a chart like the one below to write your answer.

Cause	Effect

2. How can looking at a picture before you read help you get ready to read?

3. Write a sentence with the word **dwell**, a sentence with the word **resident**, and a sentence with the word **welcome**.

4. Which building interested you the most? Why?

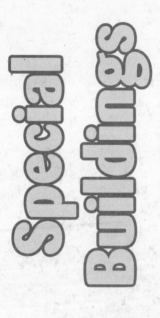

Special Buildings

by Lana Cruce

PEARSON
Scott
Foresman

Editorial Offices: Glenview, Illinois • Parsippany, New Jersey • New York, New York
Sales Offices: Needham, Massachusetts • Duluth, Georgia • Glenview, Illinois
Coppell, Texas • Ontario, California • Mesa, Arizona

16

ISBN: 0-328-13213-6

Copyright © Pearson Education, Inc.

All Rights Reserved. Printed in the United States of America. This publication is protected by Copyright, and permission should be obtained from the publisher prior to any prohibited reproduction, storage in a retrieval system, or transmission in any form by any means, electronic, mechanical, photocopying, recording, or likewise. For information regarding permission(s), write to: Permissions Department, Scott Foresman, 1900 East Lake Avenue, Glenview, Illinois 60025.

2 3 4 5 6 7 8 9 10 V010 14 13 12 11 10 09 08 07 06 05

Here's How To Do It!

1. On one piece of paper, draw a building. It could be a house, a barn, a school, a skyscraper, or any other kind of building.

2. On the other piece of paper, draw faces or other things to be on your building. They could be animals, people, objects, or anything you want. Draw things that go best with your building, like the eagle goes with the government building.

3. Cut out the pictures you have drawn.

4. Glue them onto your building, wherever you think they look the best.

15

A city has many kinds of buildings.

Wherever people **dwell,** there are buildings. Some buildings are houses. Some buildings are barns. In the city, some buildings are very tall.

Some buildings are plain. Other buildings are special. On these buildings you can see faces, beautiful flowers, and other lovely things carved out of stone. Special buildings can make a neighborhood special, too.

Now Try This

You have seen and read about many interesting buildings. Now you get to design a building of your own. You will need two pieces of paper, crayons or markers, scissors, and glue.

Here is a building with special things on it. This building is in New York City. It is 77 stories high. A story is another word for a floor in a building, so this building has 77 floors.

The building was built by a company that makes cars. If you take a close look at the building, you will **discover** hidden shapes.

What kinds of shapes do you think you will find on this building?

This is the Chrysler building.

4

Figures and pictures on buildings are all around us. You can see them whether you are a **resident** of a city or just visiting. The next time you are walking around, look up at the buildings. Try to see something you have not seen before. Maybe you will see a face, an animal, or some strange design.

You can find a world of treasures if you just look up.

13

The top of the building looks like layers of hubcaps.

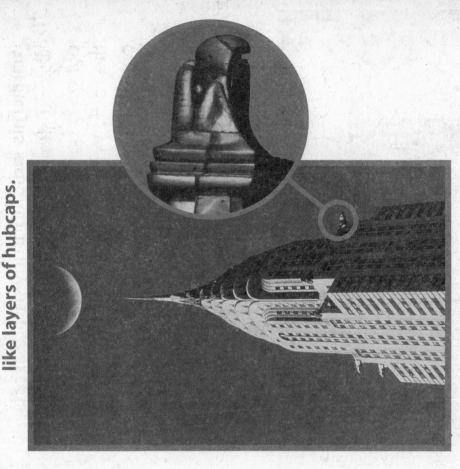

There are shapes of cars and car parts on the face of the building. Some people think the rounded parts look like hubcaps. A hubcap is a round cover that fits over the wheel of a car.

Do you see the eagle heads? These shapes were used on the hoods of cars.

It is not only government buildings that have symbols of the United States. There are barns all over the United States that have our flag painted on them. Have you ever seen a barn or other kind of building that shows our flag?

The owner of this barn is proud to be an American.

Here is another building. It has a **gargoyle** on it. Gargoyles are scary-looking stone figures. They were often put on a building to help the rain run off the roof. When it rains, the water runs out of the gargoyle's mouth.

Some people used to believe that gargoyles could scare away bad luck. Would you like to live in a building that has gargoyles on it?

This building shows an eagle on the entrance. Can you guess why? This is a **government** building. You can see a lot of government buildings with eagles. The eagle is our national bird. It is a symbol of courage and strength.

The bald eagle is a symbol of America.

One famous building where you can see many gargoyles is in Washington, D.C. It is a large church. It took more than 80 years to build this building.

There are many different kinds of stone creatures on this building. You can see strange-looking people, monkeys, fish, dogs, and elephants.

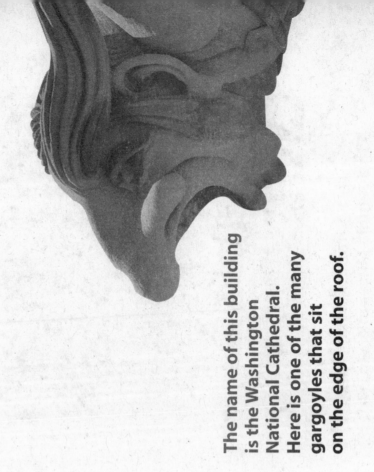

The name of this building is the Washington National Cathedral. Here is one of the many gargoyles that sit on the edge of the roof.

Here is a school building. What special thing do you think would be good for a school building? This school has a picture of the Earth painted on a brick wall. The people who built the school wanted something nice to **welcome** children to the school.

Schools often use friendly figures or pictures to make children feel welcome.

One stone decoration is a **griffin**. This one is on the roof of a museum in Philadelphia. A griffin is a made-up animal. Its front half is an eagle, and its back half is a lion. The griffin is supposed to be very strong and smart. Why do you think they put a griffin on this building?

This griffin is on the Philadelphia Museum of Art.

Look at the gargoyles on this page. What do they look like to you?

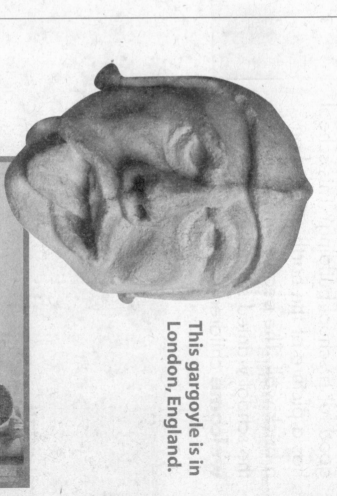

This gargoyle is in London, England.

The Ant and the Grasshopper

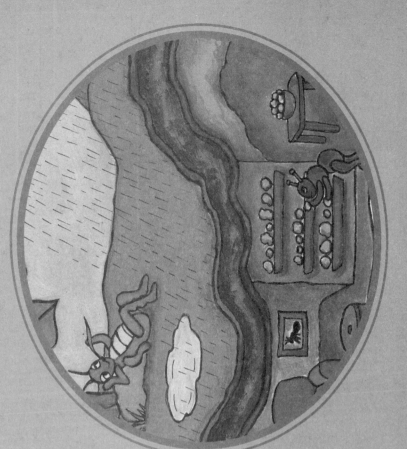

retold by Beatrice Reynolds

illustrated by Freddie Levin

Genre	Comprehension Skills and Strategy	
Fable	• Character, Setting, Plot • Cause and Effect • Story Structure	

Scott Foresman Reading Street 1.5.1

PEARSON

Scott
Foresman

scottforesman.com

Vocabulary

clever
intend
predicament

Word count: 664

Think and Share

1. Who are the characters in the story? List the ways they are different.

2. How does the grasshopper act at the beginning of the story and in the middle of the story? How does he act at the end of the story? Use a chart like this to organize your ideas.

Beginning	
Middle	←
End	←

3. On a separate sheet of paper, write at least five action words [verbs] from the book that end in –ed or –ing. Next to each word, write the base word.

4. Do you think the ant did the right thing by not giving the grasshopper some food? Why or why not?

The Ant and the Grasshopper

retold by Beatrice Reynolds

illustrated by Freddie Levin

PEARSON

Scott Foresman

Editorial Offices: Glenview, Illinois • Parsippany, New Jersey • New York, New York
Sales Offices: Needham, Massachusetts • Duluth, Georgia • Glenview, Illinois
Coppell, Texas • Ontario, California • Mesa, Arizona

Read Together

Fables

"The Ant and the Grasshopper" is a special kind of story called a *fable*. Fables are meant to teach lessons on how to behave. These lessons are called *morals*. The moral of "The Ant and the Grasshopper" is that it is important to work and to plan ahead for the future.

A man named Aesop made up the story of "The Ant and the Grasshopper." He lived more than 2000 years ago in Greece. Aesop made up many other fables as well. What is your favorite fable?

16

16 © Bettmann/CORBIS

ISBN: 0-328-13216-0

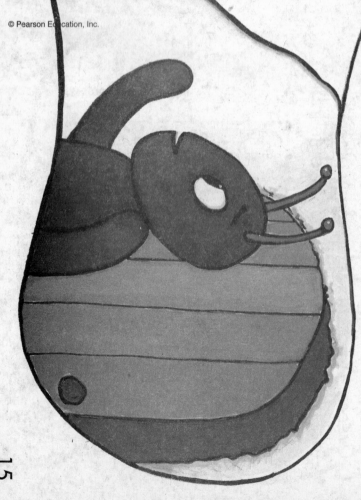

"You spent the whole summer singing and dancing while I worked," the ant said. "You even made fun of me for working so hard. Now, you want me to give you some food! I'm sorry, but I do not have enough for both of us. I hope you have learned a lesson—there is a *time to work and a time to play.*"

The ant shut his door, and the grasshopper walked away slowly. He hoped he would find some food.

So the grasshopper knocked at the ant's door. "Hello, my good friend!" he said to the ant. "I am very cold and hungry, and there is no food to be found. Will you give me something to eat?"

The ant looked at the grasshopper and shook his head.

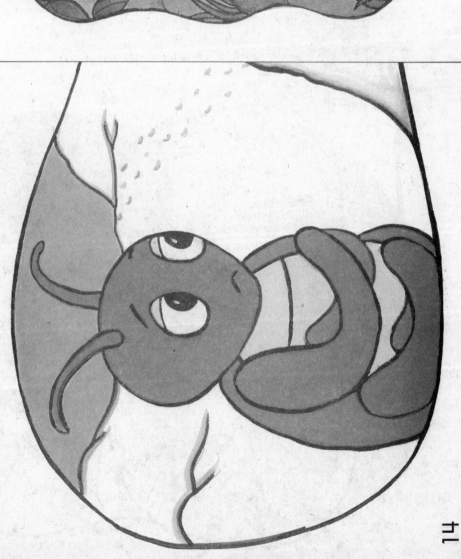

Long, long, long ago, at the edge of a field, there lived an ant and a grasshopper. The ant was a hard worker. Each summer morning, he woke up early to gather food. The grasshopper, however, was very different from the ant. He did not like to work, at all!

4

The grasshopper liked to sleep until late in the morning. Then he would spend the day dancing and singing.

The ant was always up before dawn. All day long, he carried food into his underground home. Back and forth he went, many, many times.

13

The grasshopper was sitting beneath a bare tree. He was shivering and hungry, but there was no food to be found. "Oh dear, what a predicament I am in!" he said aloud. "What shall I do? This is no fun at all!"

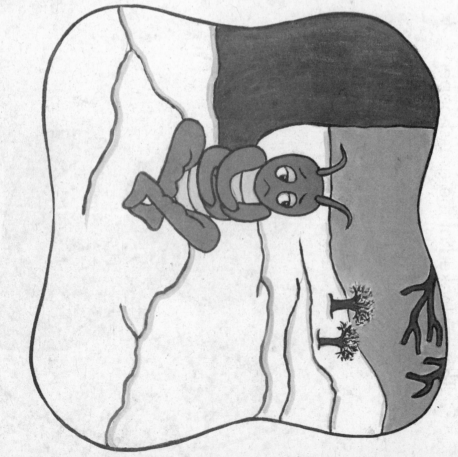

The grasshopper watched the ant work. He watched for a long time. The ant worked very, very hard. Finally the grasshopper spoke.

"I have been watching you!" the grasshopper said. "You are such a silly and dull ant! You work much too hard! Why don't you come and have a good time with me? We can sing and dance together! You need to relax and have some fun!"

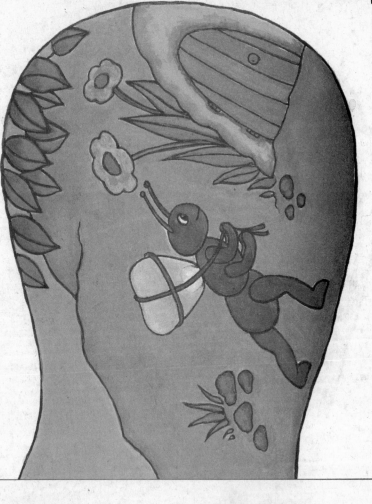

One week later, winter arrived with a big snowstorm. The ant was in his home, feeling warm and cozy. He put his feet up and made himself comfortable. "I can relax now because I have plenty of food for the long, cold winter," he thought with a smile.

"Now is not the time to play," the ant replied. "Summer will soon be over. I am gathering food for the winter, and you should do the same! How do you intend to eat during the long, cold winter months?"

The grasshopper ignored the ant. "What does he know?" the grasshopper thought. "I'm the clever one because I'm having fun. All he does is work! How very dull, indeed!" The grasshopper continued to dance and sing as the leaves fell from the trees.

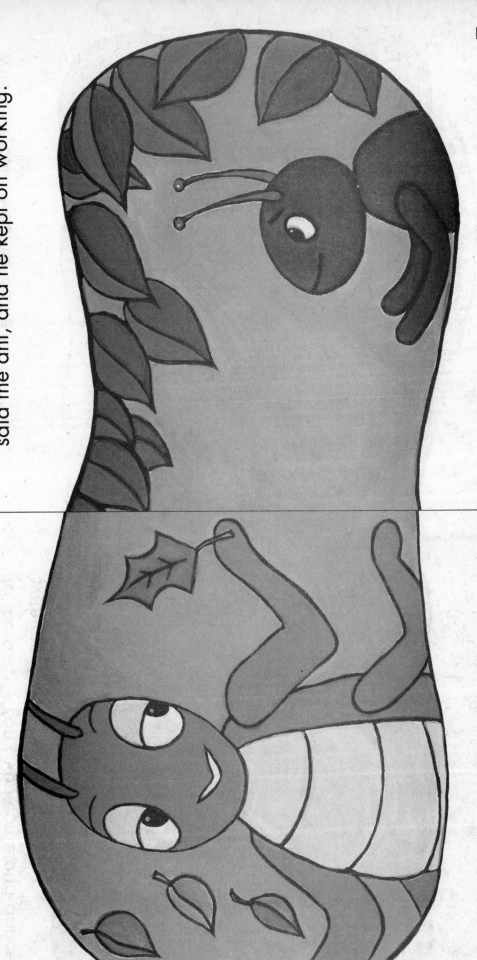

"Winter is such a long way off!" the grasshopper said. "I have enough food to eat now. I am not going to worry about winter yet. It is such a beautiful day! Are you sure you want to spend it working?"

"I can enjoy the day while I work," said the ant, and he kept on working.

"You would do well to stop dancing and start gathering some food for yourself!" said the ant. "Can't you see that winter is coming soon? What will you do when snow covers the ground, and there is no food to be found?"

On days when it rained, the grasshopper sat under a big, leafy plant. He munched on pieces of grass as he watched the rain come down.

Meanwhile, the ant was busy inside his home. He organized and stored his food so that everything would be ready when the cold weather came.

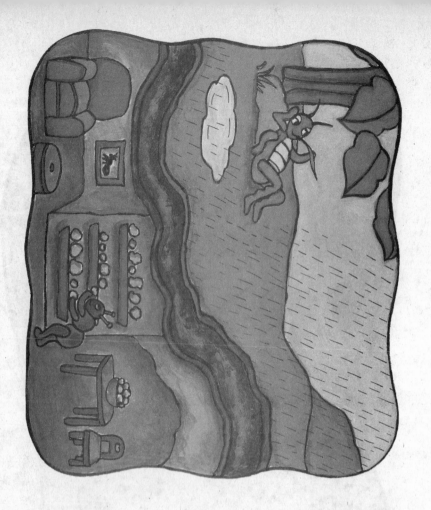

As summer turned to fall, the air got cooler.

"Winter will be here before I know it!" thought the ant. So he worked even harder than he did before.

The grasshopper kept on singing and dancing. "You are so boring!" he said to the ant. "Won't you come and dance with me?"

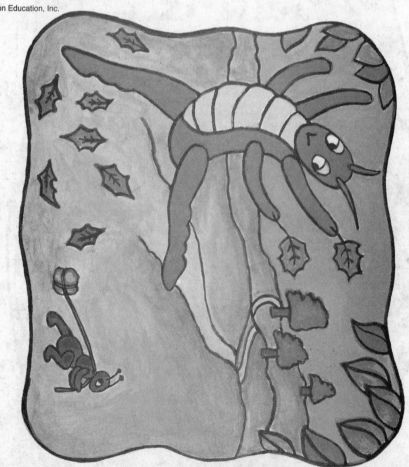

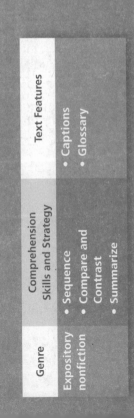

Social Studies

MAKING THE WORLD A BETTER PLACE

by Marc O'Brian

Suggested levels for Guided Reading, DRA™, Lexile® and Reading Recovery™ are provided in the Pearson Scott Foresman Leveling Guide.

Genre	Comprehension Skills and Strategy	Text Features
Expository nonfiction	• Sequence • Compare and Contrast • Summarize	• Captions • Glossary

Scott Foresman Reading Street 1.5.2

ISBN 0-328-13219-5

PEARSON

Scott Foresman

scottforesman.com

Vocabulary

aquarium

citizen

community

freedom

miserable

selfish

teenager

tutor

Word count: 544

Note: The total word count includes words in the running text and headings only. Numerals and words in chapter titles, captions, labels, diagrams, charts, graphs, sidebars, and extra features are not included.

Think and Share

1. Make a chart like the one below. Tell what you did when you were three to help. Tell what you can do now. Tell what you will do as a teenager to be a good citizen.

3 Years Old	6 Years Old	Teenager

2. How would you explain how to do the Good Citizen Project to somebody else?

3. Look at the words in the glossary. Choose four of them, and write a sentence for each.

4. Look back in the book at page 12. Tell why it is important to vote.

MAKING THE WORLD A BETTER PLACE

by Marc O'Brian

Editorial Offices: Glenview, Illinois • Parsippany, New Jersey • New York, New York
Sales Offices: Needham, Massachusetts • Duluth, Georgia • Glenview, Illinois
Coppell, Texas • Ontario, California • Mesa, Arizona

Glossary

aquarium *n.* a place to keep fish and other sea life

citizen *n.* a member of a place

community *n.* a group of people who live in the same area

freedom *n.* the right to say and do what you want

miserable *adj.* sad or unhappy

selfish *adj.* to put one's own needs and wants first

teenagers *n.* people who are between thirteen and nineteen years old

tutor *v.* to teach one child at a time

16

ISBN: 0-328-13219-5

Photo locators denoted as follows: Top (T), Center (C), Bottom (B), Left (L), Right (R), Background (Bkgd)

Cover ©Gary Braasch/CORBIS; 1 ©Tom Stewart/CORBIS; 3 ©Mark Garten/CORBIS; 4 ©William Gottlieb/CORBIS; 5 ©John Henley/CORBIS; 6 ©Gary Braasch/CORBIS; 7(T) ©David Woods/CORBIS; 7(B) ©Tom Stewart/CORBIS; 8 (T & B) ©Tom Stewart/CORBIS; 9 ©Wolfgang Kaehler/CORBIS; 10 ©LWA-Dann Tardif/CORBIS; 11(L) ©Tom Stewart/ CORBIS; 11(R) ©Ariel Skelley/CORBIS; 12 ©FRED PROUSER/Reuters/Corbis; 13 ©Bob Daemmrich/Corbis; 14 ©Hutchings Stock Photography/CORBIS

Unless otherwise acknowledged, all photographs are the property of Scott Foresman, a division of Pearson Education.

Every effort has been made to secure permission and provide appropriate credit for photographic material. The publisher deeply regrets any omission and pledges to correct errors called to its attention in subsequent editions.

2 3 4 5 6 7 8 9 10 V010 14 13 12 11 10 09 08 07 06 05

© Pearson Education, Inc.

Here's How To Do It!

1. Decide which idea you want to do for your Good Citizen Project.

2. Have your teacher help you get started with your project.

3. Then, make a book about your project. Write about what you did.

4. Tell why you did it and how it made you feel.

5. Draw pictures to go with your writing.

6. Now, share your book with others. Feel proud of what you did.

The word **citizen** means to be a member of a place. The place can be a **community**, a town, a country, or it can even be the world.

So, what does it mean to be a good citizen? For one thing, it means helping others. It means trying to make the world a better place.

Children are citizens too. In what ways can children be good citizens?

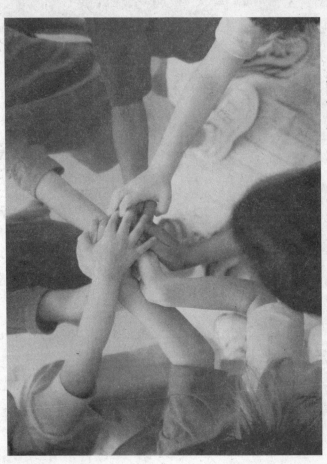

These hands are the helping hands of good citizens.

Now Try This

Here is a project that you can do with your classmates. You can work together to be good citizens at your school.

What can you do to make your school a better place? Talk with your classmates and come up with some ideas. Can you help clean up the school? Can you help with a project for younger children? How about putting artwork up in the halls?

Your teacher can write a list of all your ideas on the chalkboard.

4

Just how early can a child start being a good citizen? Well, how about at three years old?

Are you ever around three-year-olds? If you are, then you have probably heard this:

"That's mine!" and "Mommy, he's not sharing!"

No one wants to play with someone who doesn't share.

As you have read, there are many ways to be a good citizen. Here are few more ideas.

You can help rake a sick neighbor's yard. You can work with others to help clean up your neighborhood. You can give toys to children who don't have many toys.

No matter how old you are, there are many things you can do to be a good citizen and help others.

These children collected a lot of toys to give to other children.

13

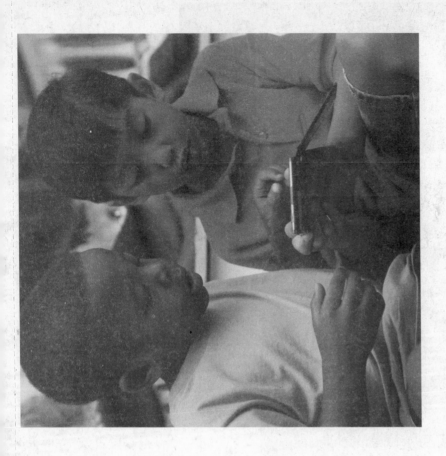

Three-year-olds have a hard time sharing and taking turns. They often want their own way. With the help of adults and older children like you, they can learn to be less **selfish**. Not sharing makes other people feel **miserable**. Learning to share is an important step toward being a good citizen.

When a teenager turns eighteen, there is something very special that they can do to be a good citizen. At age eighteen, people can vote. That means they have the **freedom** to choose leaders and help decide what laws there should be. Voting is an important part of being a good citizen.

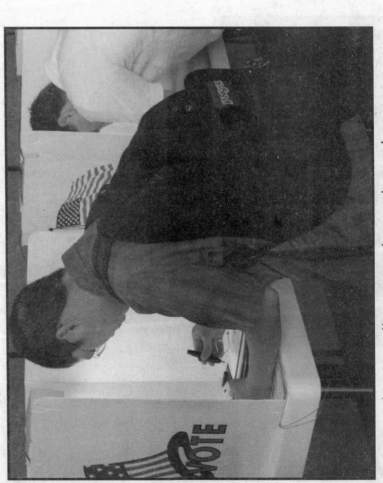

At eighteen, all citizens have the right to vote.

There are many ways that children can share and be good citizens. Some join special clubs, such as Kids Care, 4-H, or Scouts. Children in these clubs do all kinds of useful things.

Some plant trees.

Some pick up trash at the beach.

When students turn sixteen, there are even more ways to help out. These **teenagers** can go shopping for older people. They can visit people in hospitals, serve food to hungry people, and help build houses. They can even teach sports to younger children.

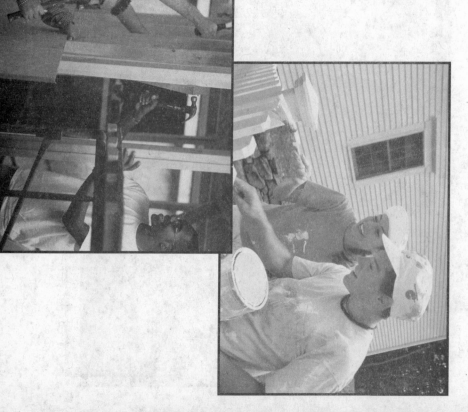

© Pearson Education, Inc.

They help clean up beaches and parks. They help plant flowers and trees. They help to take care of animals in shelters. They do many other good things as well.

Some help pick up litter.

Another popular way to be a good citizen is to **tutor** a younger child. To tutor means to teach. Older children can help younger children with math, reading, and doing projects.

Joining a club or group is not the only way to be a good citizen. You can also be very helpful on your own. Take a look at the pictures on this page. What are the children here doing to be good citizens? How are they making the world a better place?

Do you ever do any of these things?

As children grow older, there are things they can do that really interest them and help others at the same time. For example, older children who like fish and other sea creatures can help at an **aquarium**. Those who like animals can help at the zoo. They can help care for the animals and explain things to the visitors.

The Great Scientist Detectives at Work

by Ronda Greenberg

Social Studies

Suggested levels for Guided Reading, DRA™, Lexile® and Reading Recovery™ are provided in the Pearson Scott Foresman Leveling Guide.

Genre	Comprehension Skills and Strategy	Text Features
Expository nonfiction	• Compare and Contrast • Main Idea • Monitor and Fix Up	• Captions • Heads • Glossary

Scott Foresman Reading Street 1.5.3

PEARSON
Scott Foresman

scottforesman.com

ISBN 0-328-13222-5

90000

9 780328 132225

Vocabulary

explanation

fossil

investigators

record

riddle

stump

wonder

Word count: 643

Note: The total word count includes words in the running text and headings only. Numerals and words in chapter titles, captions, labels, diagrams, charts, graphs, sidebars, and extra features are not included.

Think and Share

1. How is a scientist like a detective? Use a diagram like the one below to show how they are alike and different.

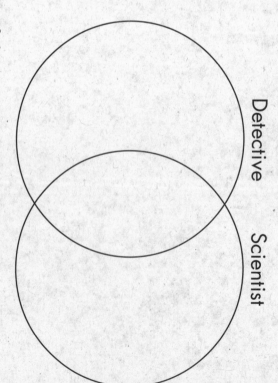

Detective   Scientist

2. If there is something you don't understand while reading, what can you do?

3. Draw a comic strip about a scientist doing an experiment. In the speech bubbles or captions, use words from the glossary.

4. Look at the pictures on pages 12 and 13. Have you ever used these tools? Tell why you used them.

The Great Scientist Detectives at Work

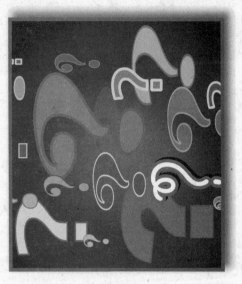

by Ronda Greenberg

PEARSON
Scott Foresman

Editorial Offices: Glenview, Illinois • Parsippany, New Jersey • New York, New York
Sales Offices: Needham, Massachusetts • Duluth, Georgia • Glenview, Illinois
Coppell, Texas • Ontario, California • Mesa, Arizona

Glossary

explanation *n.* a reason for something

fossil *n.* the remains or tracks of an animal from millions of years ago. A fossil takes the form of a rock

investigators *n.* people who find out about things

record *v.* to keep information

riddle *n.* a question that might seem to make no sense, but has a clever answer

stump *n.* the part of the tree trunk that is left when the tree is cut down

wonder *v.* to want to learn more about something

Every effort has been made to secure permission and provide appropriate credit for photographic material. The publisher deeply regrets any omission and pledges to correct errors called to its attention in subsequent editions.

Unless otherwise acknowledged, all photographs are the property of Scott Foresman, a division of Pearson Education.

Photo locators denoted as follows: Top (T), Center (C), Bottom (B), Left (L), Right (R), Background (Bkgd)

Cover ©Photodisc Collection/Photodisc Blue/Getty Image; 3 ©Photodisc Collection/ Photodisc Blue/Getty Image; 4 ©Rich Meyer/Corbis; 5 ©George Disario/Corbis; 7 ©Tom Bean/Corbis; 8 ©Raymond Gehman/Corbis; 9 ©Siede Preis/Photodisc Green/Getty Images; 10 (TR) ©Anna Clopet/Corbis, 10 (BL) ©Andy Caulfield/Photographer's Choice/ Getty Images; 11 (TR) ©Lester Lefkowitz/Corbis, 11 (BL) ©Wolfgang Kaehler/Corbis; 12 (TR) ©Royalty-Free/Corbis, 12 (BL) ©Jose Luis Pelaez, Inc./Corbis; 13 (TR) ©Reza Estakhrian/Stone/Getty Images, 13 (BL) ©Roger Ressmeyer/Corbis; 14 ©Royalty-Free/ Corbis; 15 ©Tim McGuire/Corbis.

ISBN: 0-328-13222-5

2 3 4 5 6 7 8 9 10 V010 14 13 12 11 10 09 08 07 06 05

Here's How to Do It!!

1. Shake the bag to hear how many items are in the bag and what kind of noise they make.

2. Smell the bag.

3. Feel the bag for the shape of the items.

4. Open the bag (BUT DO NOT LOOK INSIDE) and feel the items inside the bag.

5. Guess what the items are.

6. Open the bag, look inside, and see if the guess is correct.

7. Now it is your partner's turn to make a new mystery bag, and it is your turn to be a scientist and use your senses to solve the mystery of what is in the bag.

What does a detective do?

A detective looks at mysteries and then figures out what happened. Sometimes a detective predicts, or guesses about, what might happen next.

How do detectives solve mysteries? They search for an **explanation** for things that happened. They look for clues, ask a lot of questions, and pay close attention to the answers.

Now Try This

In this book, you learned that scientists, like detectives, use their five senses to solve mysteries. Now you will get to use your own senses to solve the mystery of what is in a bag. You will play this game with a partner.

You and your partner will take turns making a mystery bag and guessing what is in it. It is important that you do not peek while your partner is putting the mystery items in the bag.

You will need:
- A brown paper bag.
- Two or three mystery items to put in the bag. These can include pieces of fruit, nuts in or out of their shell, vegetables, coins, or erasers.

Close your bag with tape. Give the bag to your partner. This is what your partner should do.

This police officer asks a girl about something she saw on her way home from school.

Who can be a detective?

Some detectives are police officers. They solve crimes. They find out who broke the law. They also help find missing and stolen things.

Some detectives are private **investigators.** People hire them to find out where something or someone might be.

A tape recorder is good for recording what people say when you ask them a question. You can also talk into it yourself to record information and ideas.

With a camera you can take pictures of what you are seeing. Then you can examine the pictures later or use them to show others what you have found.

Scientists and detectives have different kinds of mysteries to solve. But they both work very hard to find the answers to their questions. And these answers will often help a lot of people.

Do you think that being a detective or a scientist sounds like something you would like to do?

There is also another person who is a kind of detective. That person is a scientist.

Just like a detective, a scientist often figures out what has happened, why it happened, and what might happen next.

This person is a scientist. She is asking herself questions about what happened to the liquid in the test tube.

How do scientists and detectives record information?

Both scientists and detectives must remember what they've learned and what questions they need to ask. They use tools to **record** the information.

Look at these pictures. These are some tools that scientists and detectives use. Do you ever use any of these tools to record information?

A notebook is very handy. You can write in it or draw pictures wherever you are.

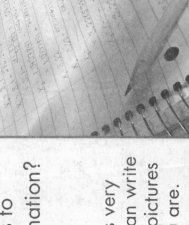

A computer is a very good place to organize information that you have found.

Detectives often start with one big question, such as *What happened?* or *What caused the accident?*

Scientists also have big questions, such as *How does your brain work?* or *What will tomorrow's weather be like?*

Just like detectives, scientists must look for clues that will help them find the answers to their questions. They study the clues to find facts—information that is known to be true.

Some scientists work with food. For example, scientists can make flavors for gum or candy. They taste the flavors to see if they are good.

This scientist is trying to make banana bubble gum.

Other scientists work with animals. Listening to the sounds the animals make can help the scientist know how an animal is feeling.

This bird is singing a happy song.

There are many kinds of scientists, but they all use their senses. Have you ever done any science experiments? What senses did you use?

This scientist studies dinosaurs. He has a big question: Where did dinosaurs live?

He is looking for clues that will help him answer the question. He has found a **fossil** of an animal footprint. It looks like this track could have belonged to a dinosaur. This fossil is a clue that tells the scientist that dinosaurs might have once lived where the fossil was found.

Scientists look for facts that help answer their questions.

There are many other ways that scientists use their senses to answer questions.

If they **wonder** what a liquid is, they might sniff it to see what it smells like.

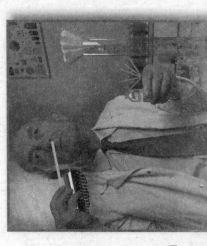

This scientist can tell that the liquid in the jar smells sour.

Some scientists are interested in stones. They might feel a stone to find out what kind of stone it is.

Sandstone is soft enough to scratch with your fingernail.

What do scientists study?

Both scientists and detectives use their five senses when they are looking for clues. The five senses are seeing, hearing, tasting, touching, and smelling.

In the picture above, the scientist is in the woods. He wants to find out about the weather long ago. He will use one of his senses to find the answer. Which sense do you think he will use?

There are many ways to find out what the weather was like. One way is to look for clues in the trunk of a tree. That is what this scientist is doing.

See the rings on the tree **stump?** Trees grow a new ring every year. So the rings on a tree can tell how old a tree is. They can also tell how much it rained in the place where the tree lives.

If the ring is big, it means there was a lot of rain that year, and the tree grew a lot. If the ring is thin, it means there was not a lot of rain that year, and it didn't grow very much.

Look at the rings. Can you answer the **riddle** of how the weather changed from year to year? Which of the five senses did you use to find the answer?

This photo shows the rings of a tree.

Simple Machines in Compound Machines

Science

Science

by Oliver García

Genre	Comprehension Skills and Strategy	Text Features
Expository nonfiction	• Main Idea • Cause and Effect • Summarize	• Heads • Labels

Scott Foresman Reading Street 1.5.4

PEARSON

Scott Foresman

scottforesman.com

ISBN 0-328-13225-X

90000

9 780328 132256

Vocabulary

compound machines

convenient

equipment

force

gadget

simple machines

Word count: 856

Note: The total word count includes words in the running text and headings only. Numerals and words in chapter titles, captions, labels, diagrams, charts, graphs, sidebars, and extra features are not included.

Think and Share

1. What is the main idea of the section of the book about simple machines? What is the main idea of the section about compound machines? Fill in a chart like the one below.

Type of Machine	Main Idea
Simple	
Compound	

2. Summarize the main ideas of this book.

3. Find the word *convenient* in the glossary and read its definition. Then use the word in a sentence about a machine.

4. What is the difference between a simple machine and a compound machine?

Simple Machines in Compound Machines

by Oliver García

Editorial Offices: Glenview, Illinois • Parsippany, New Jersey • New York, New York
Sales Offices: Needham, Massachusetts • Duluth, Georgia • Glenview, Illinois
Coppell, Texas • Ontario, California • Mesa, Arizona

Here's How To Do It!

Follow these five steps to create your own compound machine.

1. Think about what you want your machine to do.

2. Think about which simple machines can help.

3. Draw a picture of your machine. Label the parts.

4. Write about your machine. Write two to three sentences explaining what it can do.

5. Name your machine!

15

Look at the things in the picture. Do you know how they are all alike? They are all machines. A machine is anything that makes work easier.

Some of the machines in the picture are very simple. They work with just one movement. They are called **simple machines**.

Some of the machines are not so simple. They are made of two or more simple machines. They are called **compound machines**.

Now Try This

There are many different kinds of compound machines that make our lives easier and more fun.

Bikes, buses, fans, staplers, toys, and even can openers are all compound machines. They help us push, open, or lift things. They help people and things get from one place to another. They make our lives better.

All machines were invented by someone. Now it is your turn. Invent a compound machine that will help you do something. Use some of the simple machines that you read about in this book.

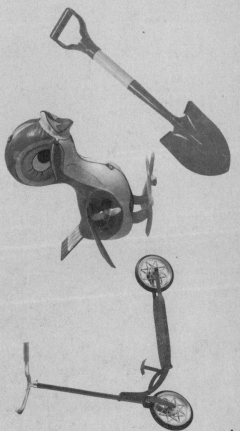

Simple Machines

We use simple machines and compound machines every day. Let's start with simple machines. There are six simple machines. Take a look at the picture. It shows you what they are.

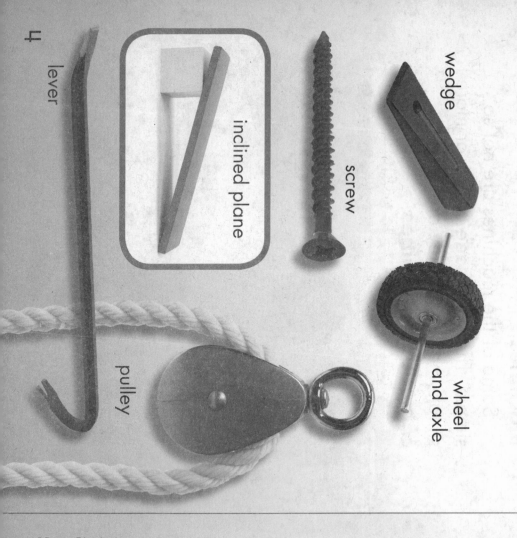

wedge

screw

inclined plane

wheel and axle

pulley

lever

Another **convenient** piece of **equipment** is a wheelbarrow. A wheelbarrow is a compound machine. It has two simple machines in it.

As you read earlier, the handles of the wheelbarrow are levers. If you pull up on them, the wheelbarrow tilts down.

Can you figure out what the other simple machine in a wheelbarrow is? It is a wheel and axle.

There are lots of other compound machines. See how many you can find around your house or school.

levers

Wheel and Axle

If you have seen a bike or a car roll down the street, then you have seen a wheel and axle in action.

The wheel and axle is a simple machine. The axle is a kind of rod, or bar, that goes through the wheel. The wheel and axle turn together and help things move.

Bikes, Ferris wheels, wagons, and cars all use wheels and axles to move.

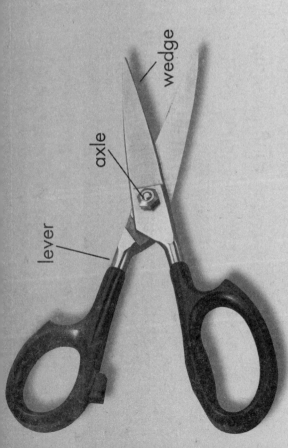

lever

axle

wedge

A pair of scissors uses levers. When you push down on the top handle of a pair of scissors, the bottom blade comes up.

A pair of scissors also uses wedges. The blades of the scissors are shaped like wedges. The blades cut through a material just like an ax cuts through wood.

A pair of scissors also uses a screw as an axle that holds the scissors together.

The three simple machines in a pair of scissors really help to make it a useful **gadget**.

Lever

Have you ever been on a seesaw? When you sit on one end, the person on the other end goes up in the air.

A seesaw is a type of lever. The lever is a very simple machine. If you push down on one end, the other end goes up. A lever can be great for lifting things.

You can also pull a lever up. When you do that, the other end goes down. That is a useful thing, too. Think of a wheelbarrow. Its handles are levers. When you lift them up, the wheelbarrow tilts down. Then you can roll the wheelbarrow.

Other levers include a shovel, a bottle opener, and a nutcracker.

What will happen if the girl pushes down on her side of the lever?

6

Compound Machines

Now that you know what simple machines are, you are ready to learn about compound machines. You may remember that a compound machine is made up of two or more simple machines working together.

Look at the scissors in the picture. Can you figure out which three simple machines are in that pair of scissors?

© Pearson Education, Inc.

11

Pulley

A pulley is another kind of simple machine used for lifting things. There are two parts to a pulley. A pulley uses a special kind of wheel. It also has something that goes around the wheel, such as a chain or a rope.

When you pull on one end of the rope or chain, whatever is attached to the other end goes up. Cranes are a kind of pulley.

Screw

The last simple machine is the screw. We use screws for joining things together. Legs are screwed to a table. Bookshelves can be screwed into walls.

Screws use an inclined plane wrapped around a small pole or tube. The inclined plane on a screw is called a thread. Threads make it easier for a screw to go up or down.

A lid on a jar of jelly is a kind of screw. When you want to close the jar, you turn the lid in a circle. Because the lid is a screw, it moves down onto the jar and closes it tightly.

thread

In one picture below, a boy is lifting a heavy box. In the other picture, a boy is using a ramp. Which do you think is easier to do?

It is easier to use a ramp. That is because it takes a lot less **force**, or energy, to push the box up a ramp than to lift it up.

A ramp is an inclined plane. An inclined plane has a flat surface, like a board. It is higher at one end than the other.

You use inclined planes to move things up or down. A ramp, a slanted road, a path up a hill, and a playground slide are all inclined planes.

© Pearson Education, Inc.

Wedge

Did you know that a knife is a machine? A knife uses a wedge to cut things. A wedge is another simple machine.

A wedge is two inclined planes joined back-to-back. It uses force to go between two things.

The head of an ax is also a wedge. It goes between the wood and splits it apart.

Telephones Through Time

by S. J. Brown

Suggested levels for Guided Reading, DRA,™
Lexile,® and Reading Recovery™ are provided
in the Pearson Scott Foresman Leveling Guide.

Genre	Comprehension Skills and Strategy	Text Features
Expository nonfiction	• Draw Conclusions • Sequence • Monitor and Fix Up	• Captions • Glossary • Map

Scott Foresman Reading Street 1.5.5

ISBN 0-328-13228-4

9 780328 132287

90000

PEARSON

Scott
Foresman

scottforesman.com

Vocabulary

automatic

determined

inventor

system

technology

Word count: 654

Note: The total word count includes words in the running text and headings only. Numerals and words in chapter titles, captions, labels, diagrams, charts, graphs, sidebars, and extra features are not included.

Think and Share

1. The phone has continued to change over the years. Why do you think this has happened?

2. Look at the pictures at the top of pages 10 and 11. How did they help you understand why Almon Strowger invented the automatic phone?

3. Pick three words from the glossary and write a sentence using each of the words.

4. Look back at the changes in phones since they were invented. Use a web to show these changes. Write the word *telephone* in the center. Draw pictures around the word to show the different kinds of phones.

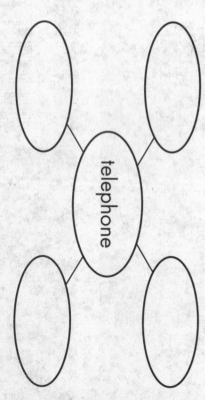

Glossary

automatic *adj.*
something that
works by itself

determined *adj.*
having one's mind
made up

inventor *n.*
someone who
designs and creates
new, useful things

system *n.* a group
of things that work
together

technology *n.*
the use of science
to improve or make
something

Telephones Through Time

by S. J. Brown

Editorial Offices: Glenview, Illinois • Parsippany, New Jersey • New York, New York
Sales Offices: Needham, Massachusetts • Duluth, Georgia • Glenview, Illinois
Coppell, Texas • Ontario, California • Mesa, Arizona

Here's How To Do It!

1. Think about what your phone will look like. What shape is it? What color should it be?

2. Remember, you can make your phone look like anything you want. You can even make it look like a toy or doll.

3. Work with your partner to make a drawing of your telephone.

4. Label the different parts and what they do.

5. Under your drawing, name your phone and tell why it is special.

6. When you are done, share your new phone invention with the rest of the class.

When you want to talk to someone who is far away, what do you do? Most likely, you pick up your telephone and make a call. These days you can call almost anybody anywhere in the world. You just push a few buttons. As you are about to learn, things were not always like that.

Now Try This

Phones of the Future

You've just learned a lot about how phones have changed over the past years. Now it's time to think about the future.

You and a partner are going to design a phone of the future. Before you and a partner begin, take some time to talk about what your phone will be like. What do you want your phone to do? Would you like to wear your phone like a ring or perhaps a watch? Your phone can do anything you want it to do— even watch a movie. Follow the steps on page 15.

New York

Boston

In 1883, phone wires were put up between New York City and Boston. Then the people in these two cities could talk to each other.

The first telephone was built by the **inventor** Alexander Bell in 1876. It used electricity to send people's voices over wires. Until then, there was no way to talk to someone in a different place.

Once the phone was invented, it didn't take long for people to want one. The first city to ever have a telephone **system** was New Haven, Connecticut. That was in 1877, only a year after the phone was invented. Other cities soon built telephone systems, as well.

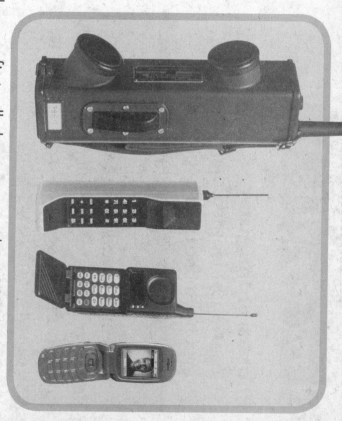

The very first cell phone was made in 1973. As time went on cell phones became much smaller and more popular. Some cell phones now let you take and send pictures to people who are far away.

As you can see, telephones—and the way we use them—have changed a lot since the days of Alexander Bell. Most likely, new kinds of telephones and new ways to use them will be invented in the future. Do you have any ideas about new telephones in the future? Perhaps you will invent one someday.

13

It would take just a few more years before people in different cities could also talk to each other.

Then, phone wires were strung across the country. People in New York could talk to someone all the way in California. By 1927, you could call someone on the other side of the Atlantic Ocean! It took weeks for a boat to travel from New York to London, England, but someone in New York could call and talk to a friend in London in less than a minute.

By 1927, someone in London, England, could call a friend who was in New York City.

London

New York

This kind of phone was first made in the 1940s. You can still find people using them today.

This unusually shaped phone was first made in the early 1960s.

This phone is called a cordless phone. People started using it in the 1980s. This kind of phone lets people move around while they talk.

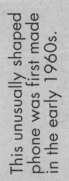

In the early 1960s there was another big change in telephones. Now, instead of dialing a number, you could push numbered buttons.

As time went on, phones continued to change. Look at the phones on this page. Have you seen these kinds of phones?

As the years went by, more and more places got telephone systems. Different kinds of **technology** were used to connect the systems. These days, almost everyone is just a phone call away.

Seattle

New York

Sao Paolo

The phone rings at the place you are trying to reach.

the operators were giving the wrong people his telephone calls. He was **determined** to do something about it.

So he invented an **automatic** phone system. With his system, a caller could dial numbers and call someone directly. People no longer needed to go through an operator.

By 1924, many people used Strowger's system instead of using operators.

This was a Strowger phone. It was made in the late 1890s. Unlike earlier phones, this phone has a dial with numbers on it.

11

Before telephones, it could take weeks or even months to communicate with friends and family in distant places. Now people who live far away can talk to each other. They can share what is happening in their lives much more easily. Is there anyone you like to call who lives far away?

Moscow

Tokyo

Johannesburg

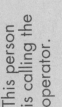

This person is calling the operator.

The operator uses a switchboard to put the call through. The switchboard allows your phone line to connect to other people's phone lines.

With early phones, you would not dial a number yourself. You picked up the receiver of your telephone and an operator would answer. The operator asked whom you were trying to reach. The operator then used special equipment to call that person for you. The pictures on these pages show you the steps that were needed to make a phone call.

In 1880, a man named Almon Strowger from Kansas City, Missouri, decided he didn't like the idea of using telephone operators. He thought that

Take a look at the picture below. Can you guess what it is? If you guessed a telephone, then you are right.

This is a picture of the first telephone. It was built by Alexander Graham Bell in 1876. It is probably much different from the phone in your house.

Telephones have changed a lot over the years. The pictures on these pages show you a few of the ways telephone technology has changed.

THIS MODEL OF BELL'S FIRST INSTRUMENT THROUGH WHICH SPEECH SOUNDS WERE FIRST TRANSMITTED ELECTRICALLY, 1875.

1877

This is the first phone that people could buy and use. People talked and listened using the same part of the phone. The part you listen at is called the receiver. The part you talk into is called the mouthpiece.

This telephone hung on the wall. On this phone the mouthpiece and the receiver are in different places.

1930

Receiver

Mouthpiece

By 1930, phones were smaller and easier to use.

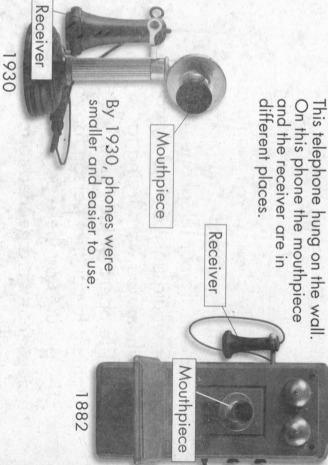

Receiver

Mouthpiece

1882

Look at these phones. What do you think of them? Notice that none of them have numbers that you can push or dial? So, how did they work? Let's find out.

Jake's Dream

by Ronda Greenberg

illustrated by Eric Reese

Genre	Comprehension Skills and Strategy	
Realistic fiction	• Theme • Sequence • Ask Questions	

Scott Foresman Reading Street 1.5.6

PEARSON

Scott Foresman

scottforesman.com

ISBN 0-328-13231-4

9 780328 132317

90000

Vocabulary

contraption

doubt

energy

Word count: 846

Think and Share

1. What was the big idea of this story?

2. Write a question you would like to ask Ben Franklin to help you understand one of his inventions.

3. Make a web with Ben Franklin in the center. Around it write the names of his inventions.

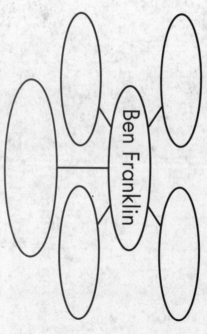

Ben Franklin

4. Go back into the story and read the description of Franklin's experiment with lightning. Tell about it in your own words.

Jake's Dream

by Ronda Greenberg

illustrated by Eric Reese

PEARSON
Scott
Foresman

Editorial Offices: Glenview, Illinois • Parsippany, New Jersey • New York, New York
Sales Offices: Needham, Massachusetts • Duluth, Georgia • Glenview, Illinois
Coppell, Texas • Ontario, California • Mesa, Arizona

Ben Franklin invented swim fins, a musical instrument called the armonica, and a special kind of eyeglasses called bifocals, as well as many other things.

In the letter to Jake, you read that Ben Franklin loved books. His first job was as a book printer. He also printed books. Later he owned his own print shop.

Ben Franklin helped many people in his day. He started the fire department in his city. He helped find ways to deliver mail more quickly. He was a man who believed in solving problems. What problems would you like to solve?

One of Ben Franklin's inventions was bifocals.

Every effort has been made to secure permission and provide appropriate credit for photographic material. The publisher deeply regrets any omission and pledges to correct errors called to its attention in subsequent editions.

16 ©Bettmann/CORBIS

ISBN: 0-328-13231-4

Jake slouched under the tree in his backyard. He was definitely having a bad day. His assignment was to come up with an idea for the "Great Ideas Fair" at his school. But Jake couldn't think of a good idea, let alone a great one.

Meanwhile, his little sister Susan was kicking dirt around the yard and moaning.

"I'm bored," she said. "Everything is boring."

Jake thought Ben Franklin certainly had come up with a lot of interesting ideas. He invented a grabber, experimented with lightning, and even started a lending library.

Again, Jake looked out the window to the yard where Susan was still fussing. He thought again about Ben Franklin's ideas. Suddenly, he knew what to do!

"I'll start a library, just like Ben Franklin," said Jake. "Only it will be a toy library. Kids can bring in their toys and trade them for different toys! It will be like having a new toy all the time, and it won't cost a cent."

His mother said, "Jake, this is an all-time great idea! You should enter the idea in the Great Ideas Fair. It's sure to make everyone happy!"

That is exactly what Jake did.

Jake did not want to listen to Susan complain, so he went up to his room and started to think about a movie he saw in school. It was about Benjamin Franklin who lived a long time ago. Ben Franklin invented many important things and had many good ideas. Jake wished Ben Franklin were around to help him with an idea right now.

"We can't buy new toys whenever you want them," said Mom. "Toys are expensive. Play with the ones you already have."

"I wish Susan would be quiet," Jake thought. "I still need to come up with an idea."

But Jake was so tired from thinking that he fell asleep and began to dream.

In his dream, Jake went down to his mailbox where he found a letter from, of all people, Ben Franklin!

Dear Jake,

I heard you were having a problem coming up with a clever idea for your Great Ideas Fair. I hate to see you feeling so bad, so I thought I would write you a letter. Maybe if I tell you about some of the things I've done, it will help you get an idea of your own.

In his dream, Jake refolded the letter and put it in his pocket. Then, he heard shouting. The shouting became louder and louder still. It woke him up!

Jake peered out the window. The shouting was coming from his sister Susan.

"All my toys are boring! I want new ones! I want an airplane for my doll to fly. I want a purple pony with pink hair. Please!" cried Susan.

You might remember that I loved inventing contraptions. One of my all-time favorite inventions is what you now call a grabber. I came up with the idea one day while trying to reach a book from a high shelf in my library.

I took a wooden pole and put a kind of claw at the end. The claw helped grab the book off the shelf. I called it the long arm. It was a simple idea that worked quite well.

I liked inventing things, but I also wanted to understand nature and the world around me, like lightning. Back in my time, nobody knew what lightning was.

I thought that lightning might have something to do with electricity. As you know, electricity is a type of energy. It makes the lights in your house go on and your TV work.

Jake, I hope you are enjoying reading my letter so far. As for me, I love to read—all kinds of books.

I wanted everyone to have books to read. But in my time, books cost a lot of money. Only very rich people could buy them. That seemed unfair. So, some friends and I put our money together and bought books.

We opened a library so that everyone could borrow books to read. It was the very first lending library in America!

Well, Jake, it's time for me to say good-bye, but I hope this letter has helped you. I believe you are a fine and clever boy, and I feel sure that you will not have much trouble coming up with a good idea.

Best of luck,
Benjamin Franklin

So on a stormy day, I tied a piece of pointed metal to my kite. Then I tied a key to the bottom of the kite string. I let my kite sail off into the wild dark sky.

The sky was full of thunder and lightning. I could feel the energy in the air. The energy from the lightning went all the way down the kite string to

the key. When I touched the key, there was a spark! The spark proved that lightning was electricity.

Electricity can be very dangerous, and lightning can kill people. I was lucky I wasn't hurt. Never try experiments with electricity without a grown-up around.

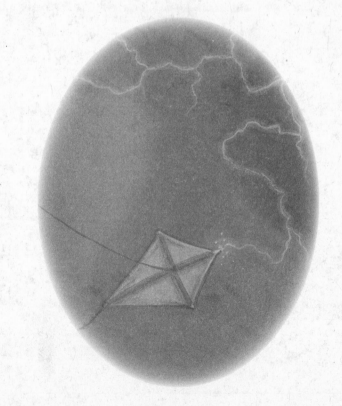